BRICK
BUILDINGS

40 CLEVER AND CREATIVE IDEAS
TO MAKE FROM CLASSIC LEGO®

KEVIN HALL

BARRON'S

A Quintet Book

First edition for the United States and Canada
published in 2017 by Barron's Educational Series, Inc.

All inquiries should be addressed to:
Barron's Educational Series, Inc.
250 Wireless Boulevard
Hauppauge, NY 11788
www.barronseduc.com

Library of Congress Control Number: 2016962958
ISBN 978-1-4380-1092-2
QTT.BKITH

This book was conceived, designed, and produced by
Quintet, an imprint of the Quarto Group
Ovest House
58 West Street
Brighton, East Sussex
BN3 1DD
United Kingdom

Designers: Anna Gatt, Michelle Rowlandson
Project Editors: Kath Stathers, Leah Feltham
Editorial Director: Emma Bastow
Publisher: Mark Searle

9 8 7 6 5 4 3 2 1

Printed in China by C & C Offset Printing Co Ltd.

welcome to BRICK BUILDINGS

A lot of the time when I am at an event displaying my
LEGO® brick models, I am asked if my models and
sculptures are created using special parts, or if I get unique
parts made especially for a particular model. The answer is
that the parts I use are the exact same parts that you get in
the LEGO sets you purchase in the stores. This book is to
show just that.

The models in this book are all based on different types
of buildings. Some are real and some are created purely
from my imagination, but they all make great use of color
and shape.

On the whole, the models have been created using the
basic parts that you will find in the CLASSIC boxes, which
of course aren't just classic 2 x 4 bricks, but include slopes,
plates, tiles, and even tiny, colorful 1 x 1 tiles. However, to
create some of the finer details of these micro buildings,
I have used parts from other LEGO sets such as Friends
and Creator. I find that 1 x 1 headlight bricks (also known as
Erling Bricks, named after their inventor, the LEGO designer
Erling Dideriksen) are very versatile. You'll see them crop up
as tiny windows or for connecting parts to the sides of walls.
Even animal horns appear in interesting places—such as at
the end of shoelaces on the Shoe House.

When I am building my models, I always love the challenge
of creating a model using the parts I have at hand. So, don't
worry if you haven't got the exact pieces I list. Just like
any LEGO builder, you can be creative and re-create the
models in this book to suit the parts you have in your own
collection. Remember, there is no right or wrong way of
building with LEGO, as long as you have fun creating the
models. That is the most important thing.

—Kevin Hall, Brick Galleria Ltd

contents

log cabin

When you're living in a forest, it makes sense to have a house made out of wood—after all, that's the building material that's most readily available. Plus, log cabins do have a certain charm. If you want your LEGO® forest to have even taller trees, just keep adding more sections of the slopes. The tiny cabin door is made from a tile placed vertically.

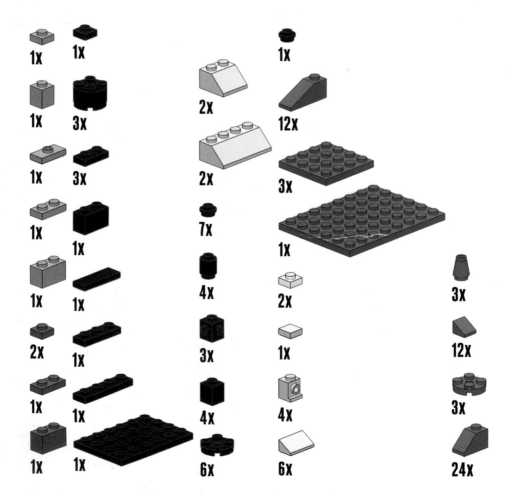

1x 1x

1x 3x

1x 3x

1x 1x

1x 1x

2x 1x

1x 1x

1x 1x

2x 1x

2x 12x

2x 3x

7x 1x

4x 2x 3x

3x 1x 12x

4x 4x 3x

6x 6x 24x

LOG CABIN

1

2

3

4

5

(MAKE 3)

6

7

8

9

10

11

12

island fortress

Every island needs a fortress to keep its inhabitants safe. Traditionally, coastal fortresses were used to protect shipping routes and to house armies so the island could be ready for an attack from the sea. These cannons are made using minifigure telescopes clipped onto 1 x 1 plates with a clip on top. The tower roofs are upside down radar dishes topped with a cone.

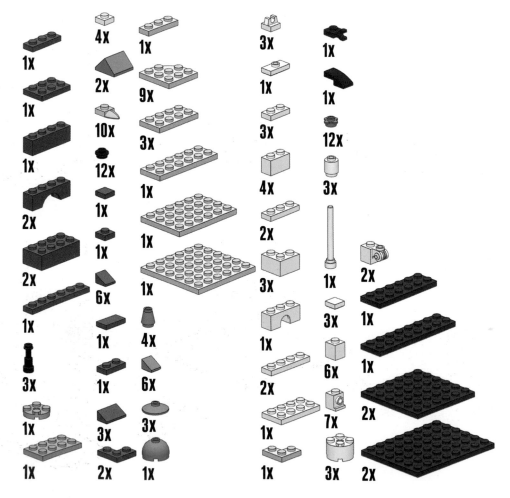

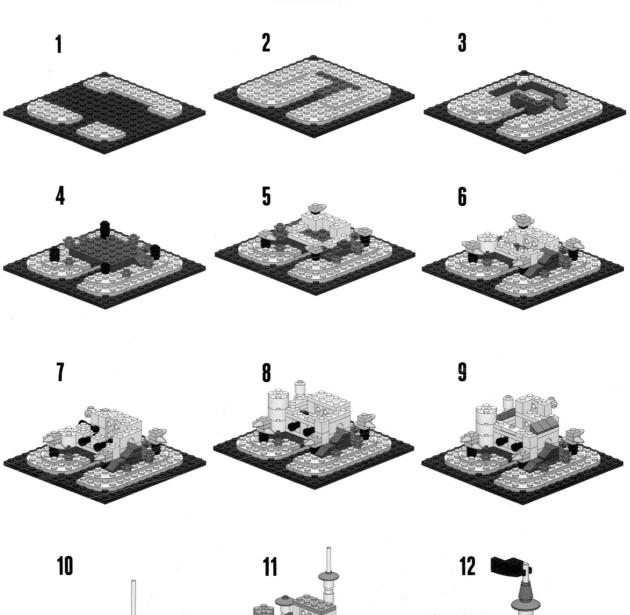

1

2

3

4

5

6

7

8

9

10

11

12

cloud house

Who hasn't daydreamed about living on a cloud? Imagine floating through the sky, chatting to the birds, and looking down at people living their lives below. I've used a variety of different curved bricks and curved slopes to give the cloud its unique fluffy look. A good trick for creating a window is to turn 1 x 1 bricks sideways in a group of four.

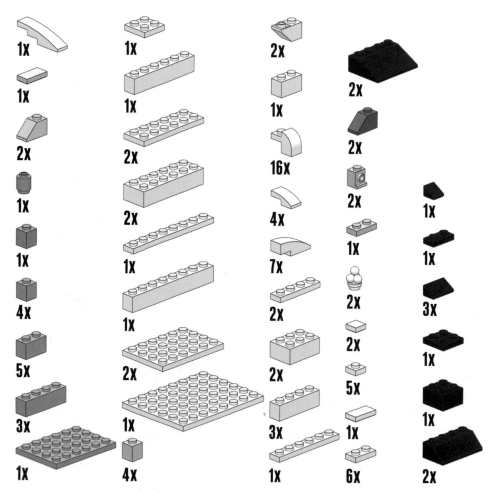

1X
1X
2X
1X
1X
4X
5X
3X
1X

1X
1X
2X
2X
1X
1X
2X
1X
4X

2X
1X
16X
4X
7X
2X
2X
2X
3X
1X

2X
2X
2X
1X
2X
2X
5X
1X
6X

1X
1X
3X
1X
1X
2X

CLOUD HOUSE

1

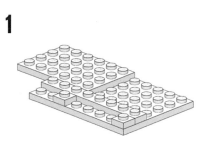

2

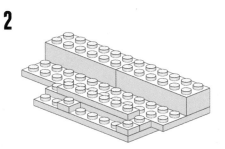

3

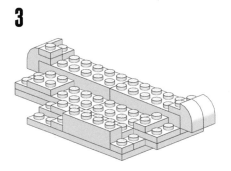

4

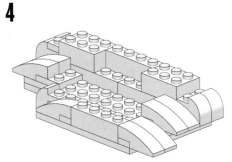

5

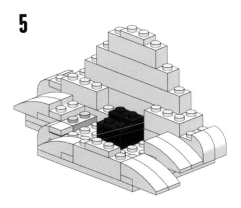

6

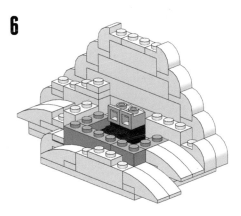

7

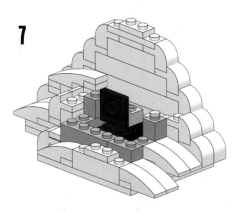

8

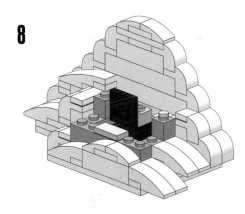

9

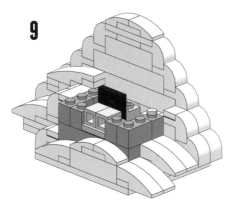

10

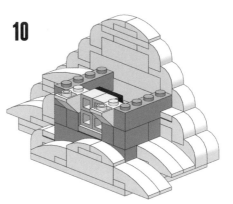

11

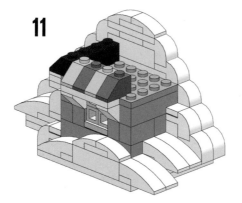

12

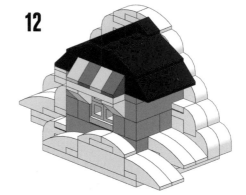

13

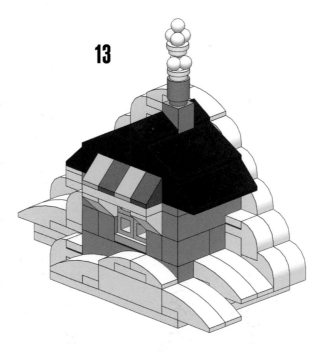

gatehouse

Gatehouses were used to guard the entrances to the grounds of many large mansions and castles. A gatekeeper would live in the house so he could check who was going in or out at all hours. The arrow slits beside the door of the gatehouse are made using 1 × 2 tiles sideways and attaching them to a 1 × 1 brick with a stud on the side. Hinge plates allow the door to open and close like a real gatehouse.

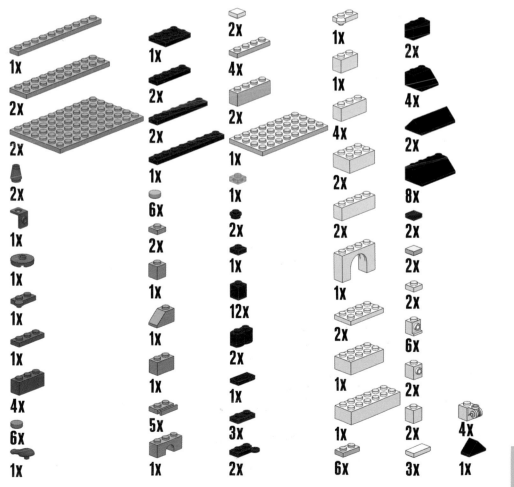

1X
2X
2X
2X
2X
1X
1X
1X
1X
4X
6X
1X

1X
2X
2X
1X
6X
2X
1X
1X
1X
1X
5X
1X

2X
4X
2X
1X
1X
2X
1X
12X
2X
1X
3X
2X

1X
1X
4X
4X
2X
2X
1X
2X
1X
1X
1X
6X

2X
4X
2X
8X
2X
2X
2X
6X
2X
2X
3X

2X
4X
2X
8X
2X
4X
1X

GATEHOUSE

1

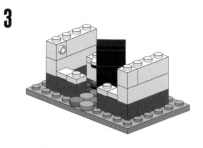

2

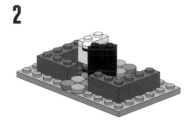

3

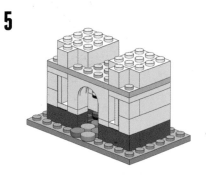

4

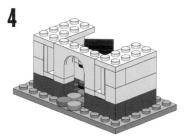

5

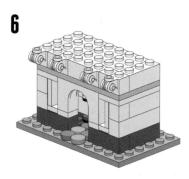

6

7

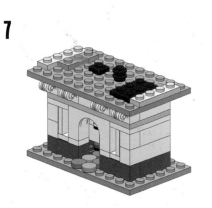

8

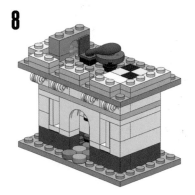

9

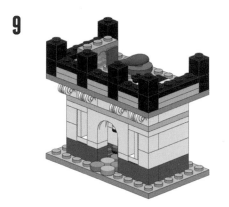

10

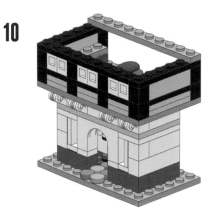

11

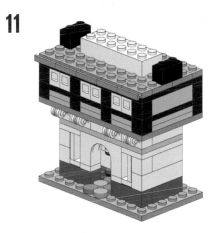

12

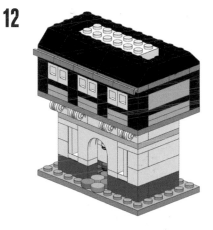

13

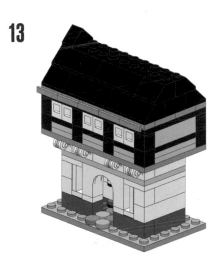

14

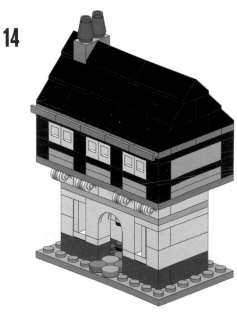

underwater house

There is a mythical city called Atlantis that is said to have sunk into the sea. As nobody has found it yet, why not build yourself your own underwater house instead? This one uses 2 x 2 round bricks with grilles to give the pillars an authentic look of ancient Mediterranean architecture. The spiky tails make great seaweed.

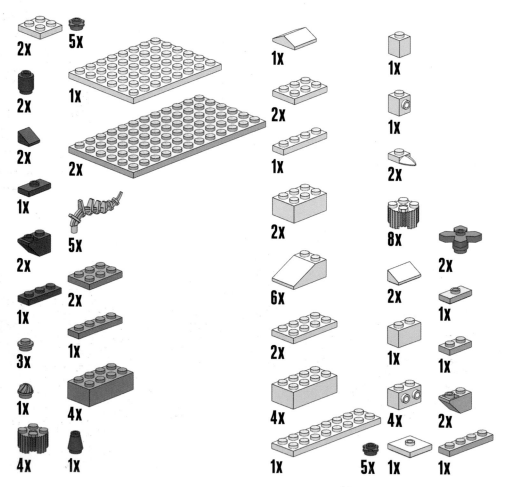

UNDERWATER HOUSE

1
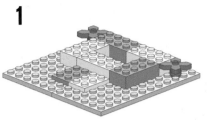

2
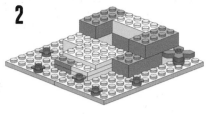

3

4
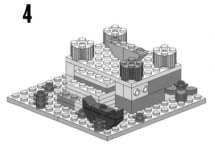

5
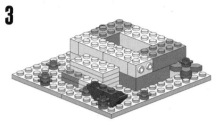

6
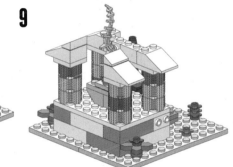

7
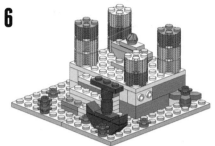

8
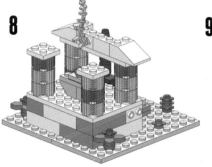

9
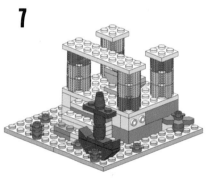

10

11

12

hollow trunk

Look inside a hollow tree trunk and you'll find the homes of any number of mini beasts. And perhaps there are tiny houses in there too, where mythical creatures such as elves might live. The trunk's solid base is made using two 2 × 3 corner slopes that make the base wider without having to use lots of bricks. Half arches are perfect for building up branches that can then be covered in foliage.

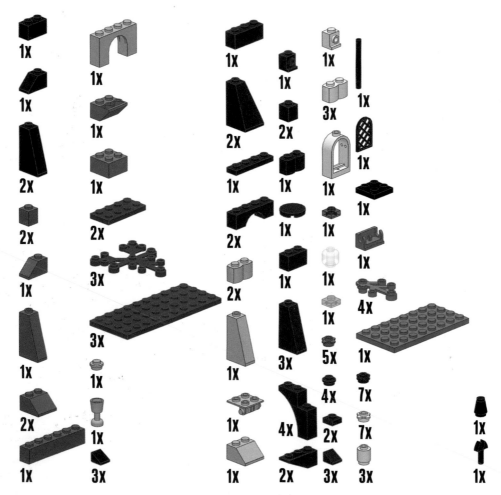

1X 1X 1X 1X 1X

1X 1X 1X 3X 1X

2X 1X 2X 2X 1X

2X 2X 1X 1X 1X

1X 3X 2X 1X 1X 1X 4X

3X 3X 5X 1X

1X 1X 4X 7X

2X 1X 1X 4X 2X 7X 1X

1X 3X 1X 2X 3X 3X 1X

18

HOLLOW TRUNK

1

2

3

4

5

6

7

8

9

10

11

12

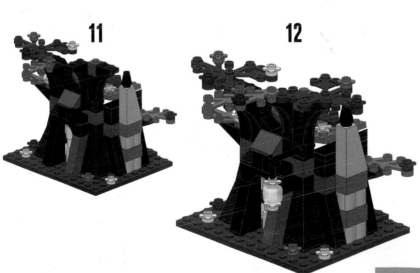

clifftop villa

Many modern houses are built on the tops of cliffs—with endless views of the sea and sunsets typically enjoyed through a large plate glass window. Using various slopes, you can create great rocky cliff faces that can be scaled up or down depending how high you want your cliff to be. The waterfall uses a combination of dark blue, pale blue, and transparent blue plates to give the impression of falling water.

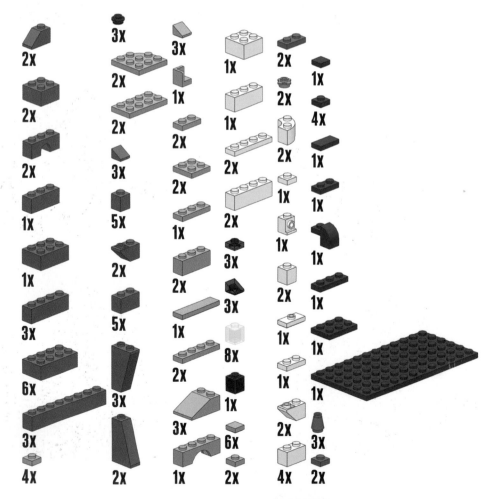

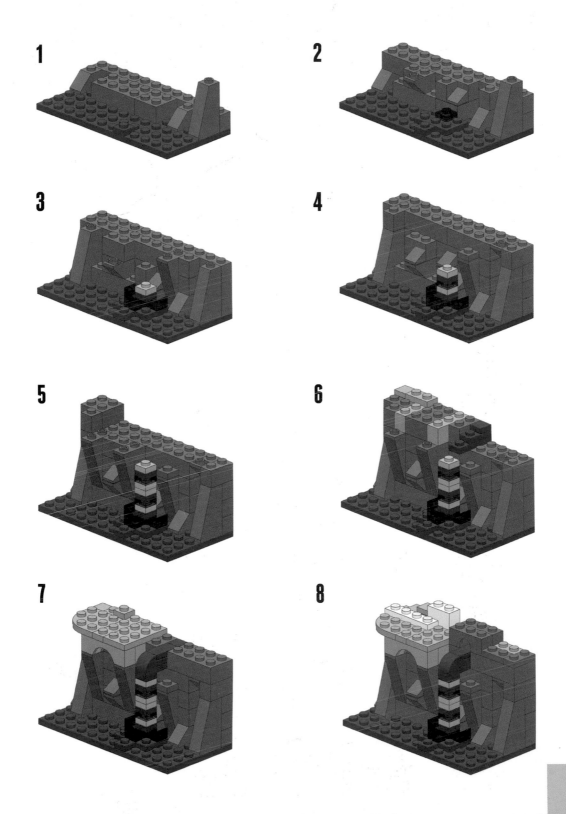

9

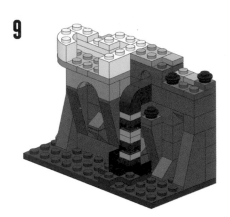

10

11

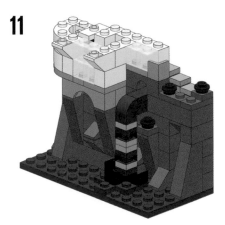

12

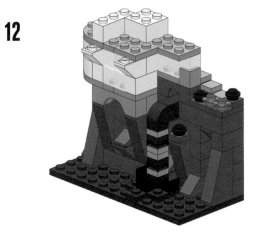

13

14

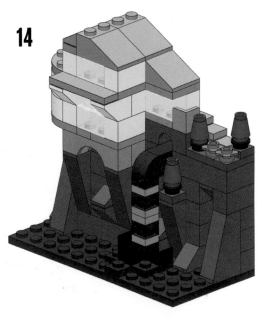

flying house

Have you ever wanted to live somewhere different? Imagine if you could just up and fly away to anywhere in the world—the beach, the jungle, the top of Mount Everest, you name it! This house has flapping wings that can bend in the middle, as well as at the point where they connect to the house.

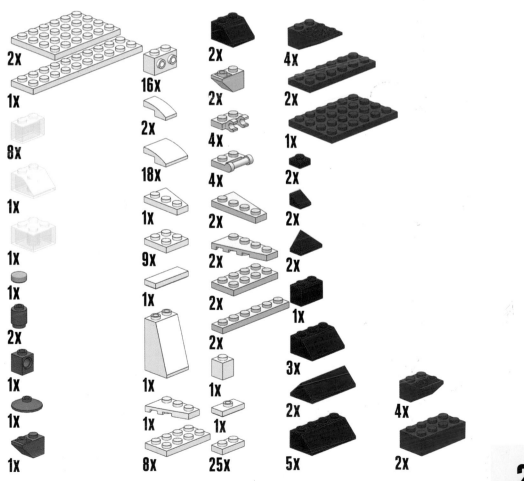

2x
1x
8x
1x
1x
1x
2x
1x
1x
1x

16x
2x
18x
1x
9x
1x
1x
1x
8x

2x
2x
4x
4x
2x
2x
2x
2x
1x
1x
25x

4x
2x
1x
2x
2x
2x
1x
3x
2x
5x

4x
2x

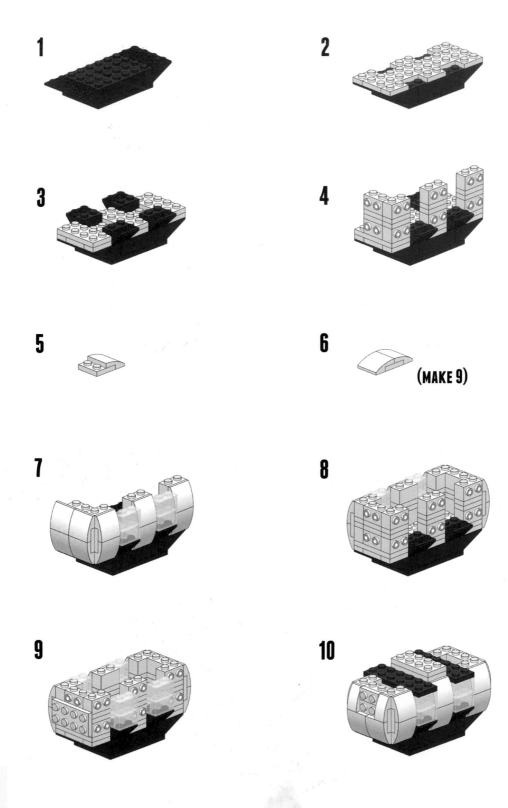

FLYING HOUSE

11

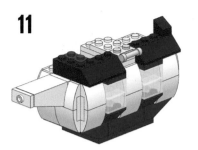

12

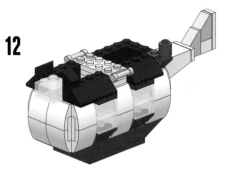

13

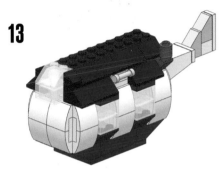

14

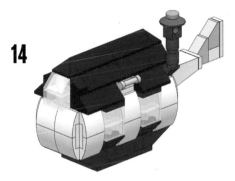

15

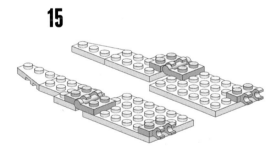

16

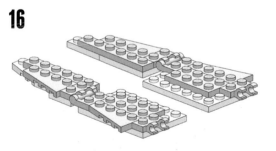

17

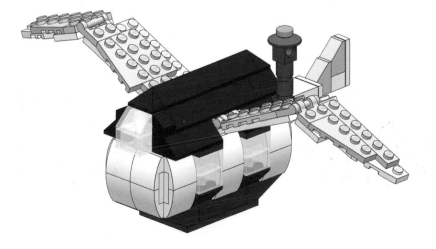

royal palace

There are palaces all over the world that were originally the official residences of kings, queens, bishops, and emperors. Many are now open as tourist attractions. In the UK, the Queen still lives in Buckingham Palace, which has 775 rooms.
The 1 x 1 headlight bricks facing inward create the uniform window pattern popular in many palaces.

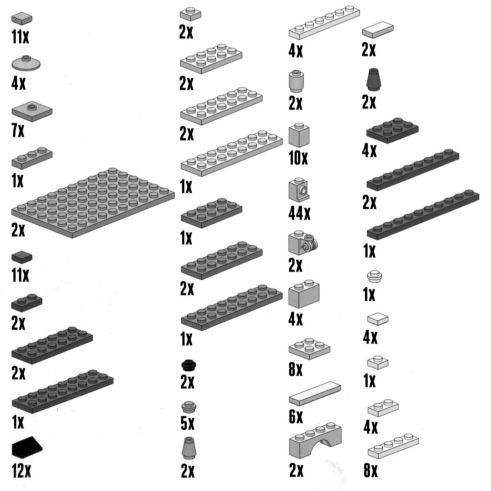

11X

4X

7X

1X

2X

11X

2X

2X

1X

12X

2X

2X

2X

1X

1X

2X

1X

2X

5X

2X

4X

2X

10X

44X

2X

4X

8X

6X

2X

2X

2X

4X

2X

1X

1X

4X

1X

4X

8X

ROYAL PALACE

houseboat

Floating on the water can be very relaxing, so imagine what living on a houseboat must be like! And you'll always be ready for a quick dip! I've used inverted slopes to create the boat's hull and made the wood paneling by putting tiles on bricks with studs on the side.

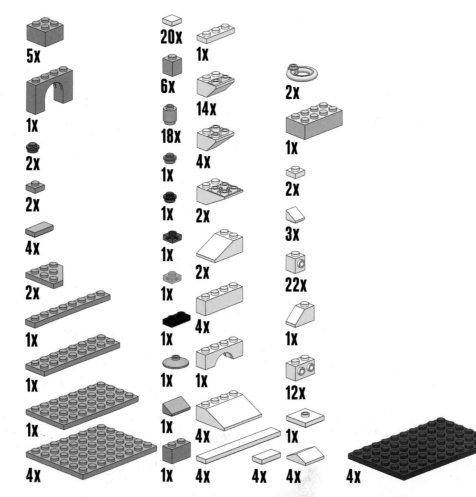

5x
1x
2x
2x
4x
2x
1x
1x
1x
4x

20x
6x
18x
1x
1x
1x
1x
1x
1x
1x
1x

1x
14x
4x
2x
2x
2x
4x
1x
1x
4x
4x
4x

2x
1x
2x
3x
22x
1x
12x
1x

4x

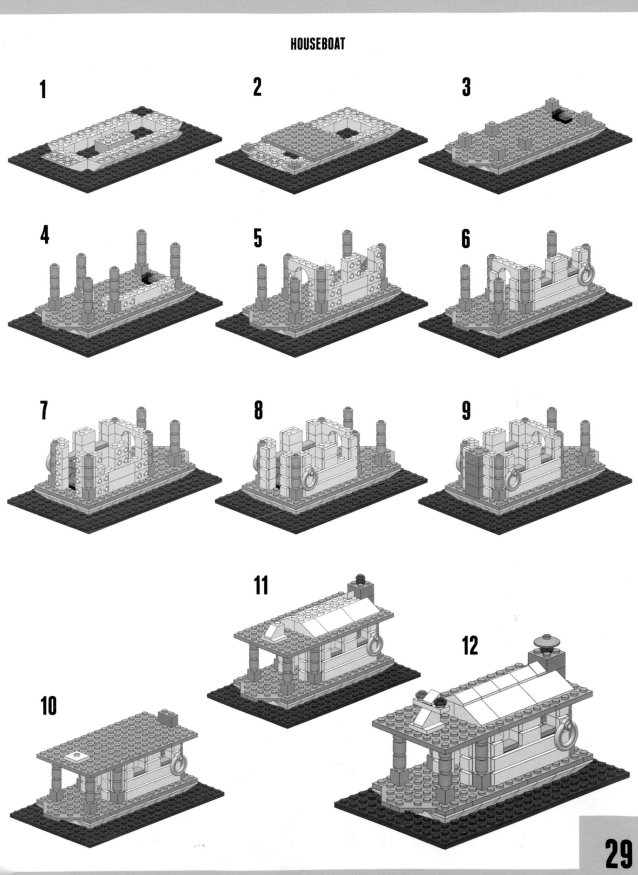

fairy house

Fairy houses are hidden in gardens or deep in the woods so that humans can't find them. They build them using natural elements, just like the roof in this house, which is made with an upside down flower. I've used wedge plates for the petals, which are normally used for wings. When angled inward, they come together to create a pitched roof. Using two different tones of orange makes the chimney look more realistic.

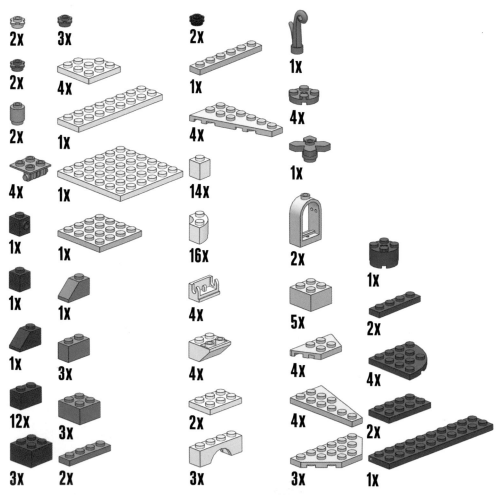

2x 3x 2x 1x

2x 4x 1x 4x

2x 1x 4x 1x

4x 1x 14x

1x 1x 16x 2x 1x

1x 1x 4x 5x 2x

1x 3x 4x 4x 4x

12x 3x 2x 4x 2x

3x 2x 3x 3x 1x

FAIRY HOUSE

1

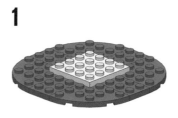

2

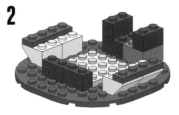

3

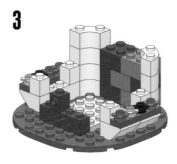

4

5

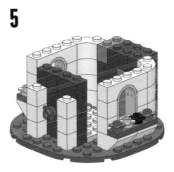

6

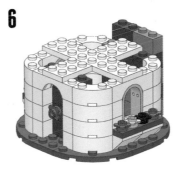

7

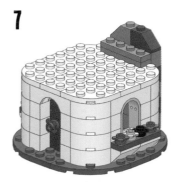

8

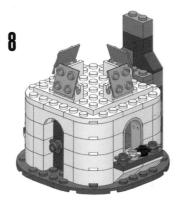

9

(MAKE 4)

10

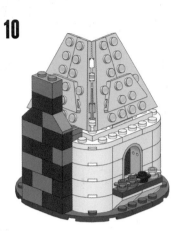

11

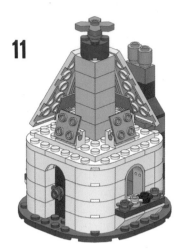

12

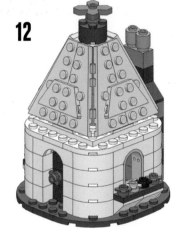

13

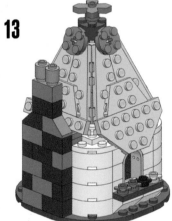

14

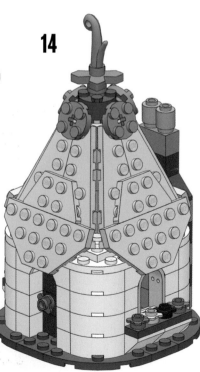

gingerbread house

You can build gingerbread houses out of real gingerbread—and then eat them all up! But that's usually a Christmas treat, so for the rest of the year you can make this one out of LEGO® bricks. I've used click hinges to give the roof the perfect slope so that plates can be placed in layers to look like icing. Alternate red and white round 1 x 1 plates make great candy canes to place at the corners of the house.

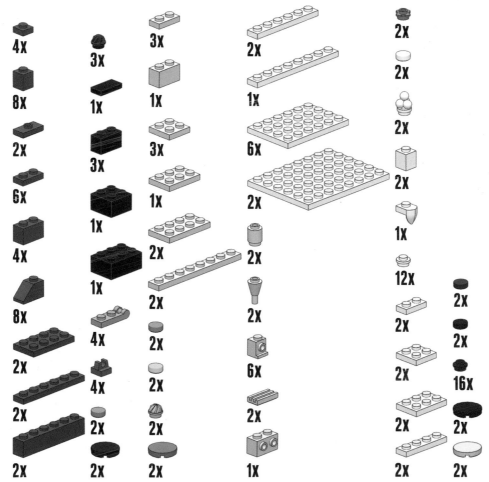

GINGERBREAD HOUSE

1

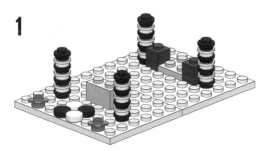

2

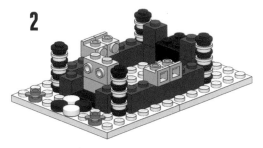

3

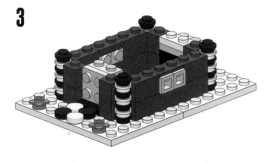

4

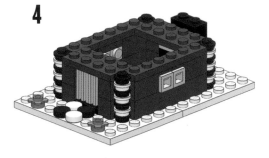

5

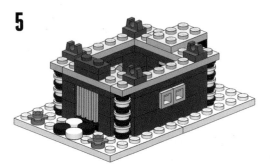

6

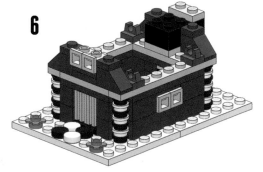

7

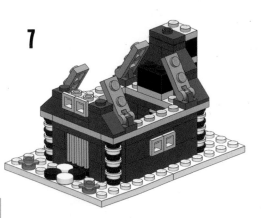

8

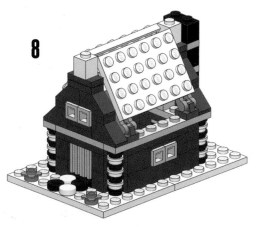

9

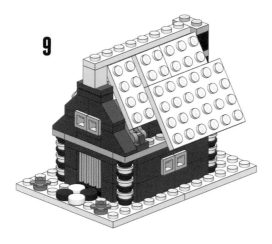

10

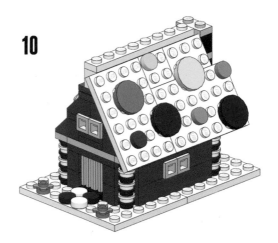

11

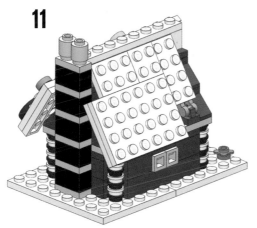

12

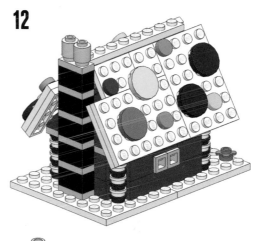

13

micro castle

Castles don't have to be big to be awesome. This micro castle can fit in the palm of your hand, but it still has all the details you need. I've used 1 x 1 and 1 x 2 panels to create the outer walls, and unicorn horns make perfect little spires to go on the top of the towers.

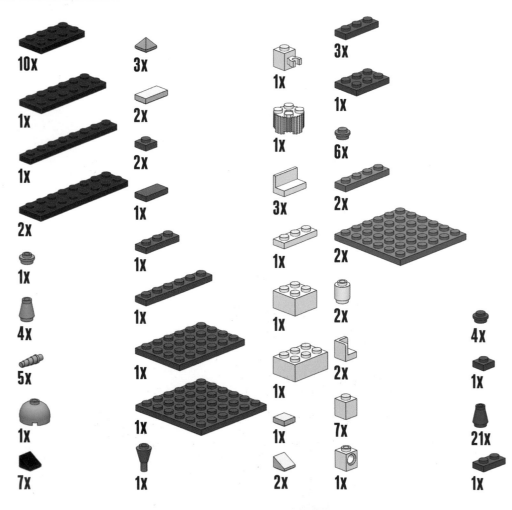

10x 3x 1x 3x

1x 2x 1x 1x

1x 2x 1x 6x

2x 1x 3x 2x

1x 1x 1x 2x

4x 1x 1x 2x 4x

5x 1x 2x 1x

1x 1x 1x 7x 21x

7x 1x 2x 1x 1x

MICRO CASTLE

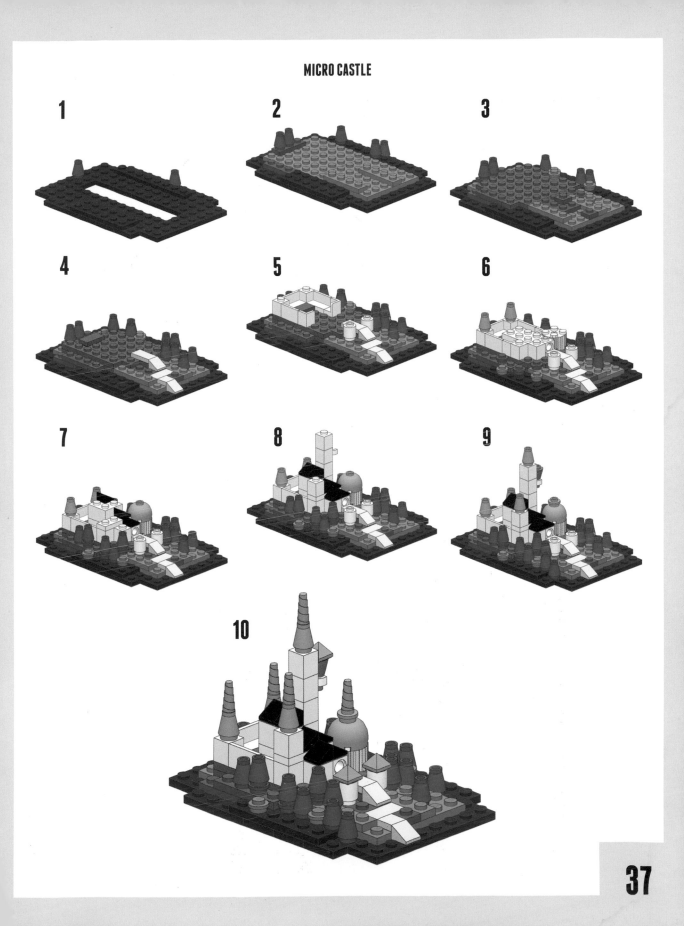

lake house

Some houses near lakes and rivers are built on pillars so that they don't flood when the water level rises. Small boats can dock right up beside them. If you were a fisherman you wouldn't have to travel far to get to work. The 1 x 2 tiles with grooves make great wood panels for the dock and the floor.

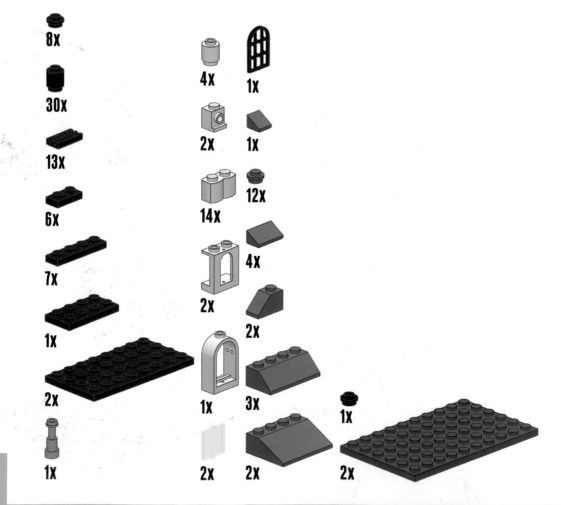

8x
30x
13x
6x
7x
1x
2x
1x

4x
2x
14x
2x
1x
2x

1x
1x
12x
4x
2x
3x
2x

1x
2x

LAKE HOUSE

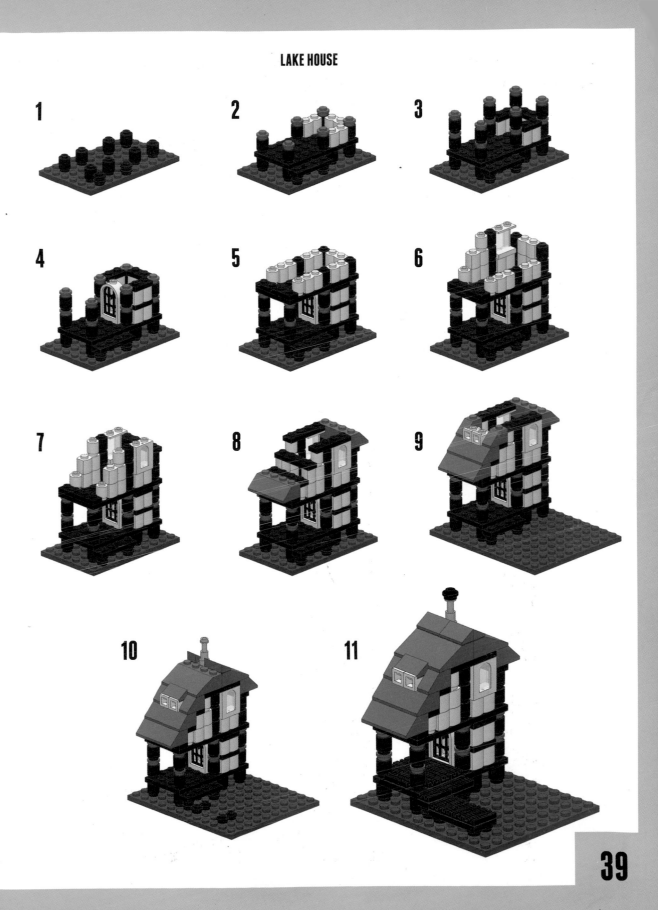

mobile home

A mobile home is a great way to travel. If you find a place you really like, you can just turn the engine off and stay there awhile. Some people live permanently in mobile homes so that they're always ready to move on when the mood strikes. The double wheels at the back need a 6 × 1 arch to span them.

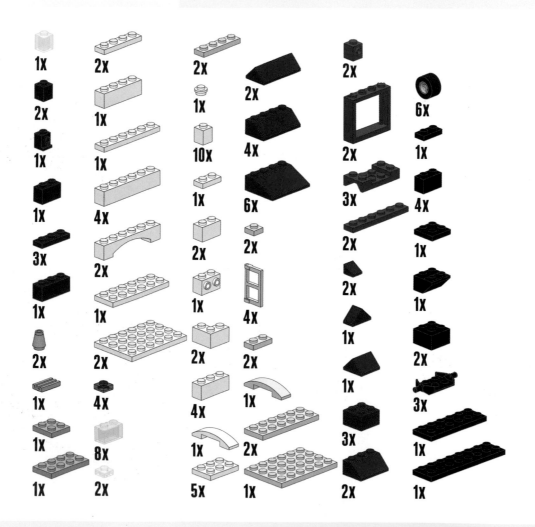

MOBILE HOME

1

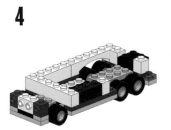

2

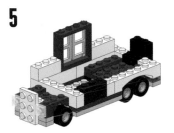

3

4

5

6

7

8

9

10

11

12

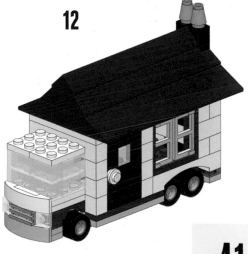

tall tower

In medieval times, towers were built as a sign of wealth—the higher the tower, the more money you had. They also make good lookout points for guarding towns from invasion, or for jails to spot prisoners who try to escape. This tower has a central core made of 1 x 1 bricks with studs on each side, then plates attached to each one.

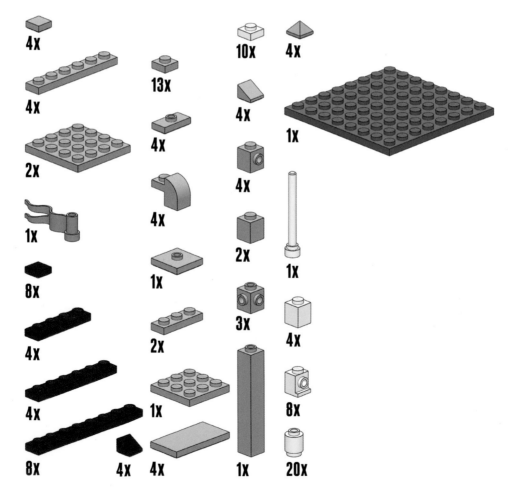

TALL TOWER

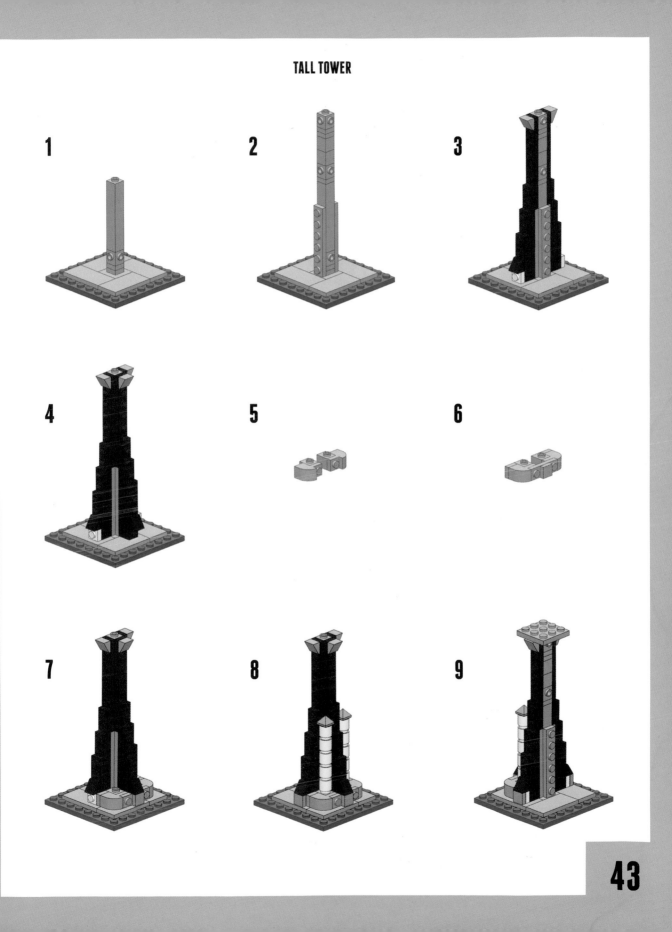

TALL TOWER

10

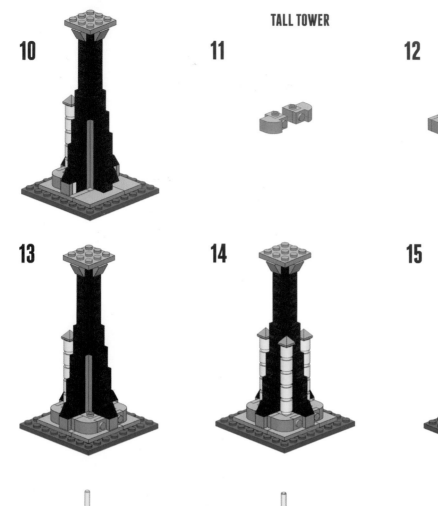

11

12

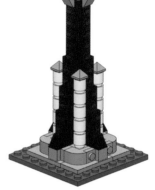

13

14

15

16

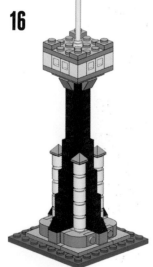

17

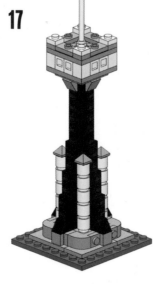

18

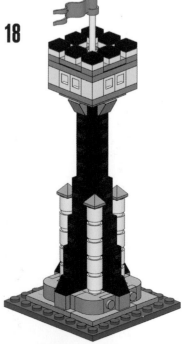

magical mill

Most mills powered by running water grind wheat or create electricity, but this magical mill creates magic when the wheel turns. Make a wish as you turn the wheel and see what happens. It uses 1 x 1 round bricks stacked together to create the axel and 1 x 3 arched bricks over the top of the axel so it can turn freely. The mill wheel is created using 1 x 1 bricks with a stud on the side that have 1 x 2 slopes attached.

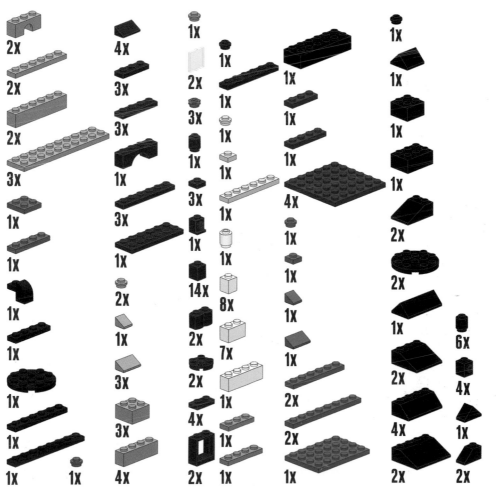

45

1

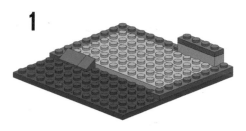

2

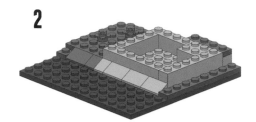

3

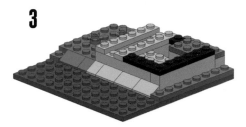

4

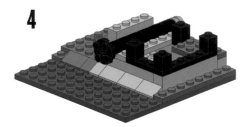

5

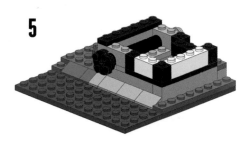

6

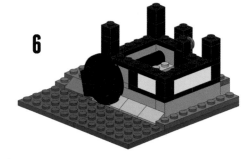

7

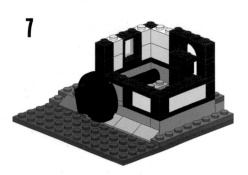

8

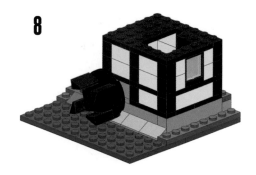

9

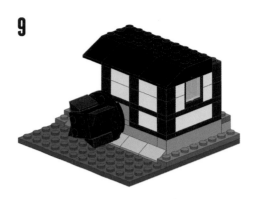

10

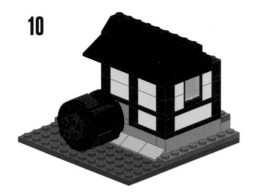

11

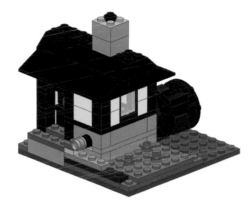

12

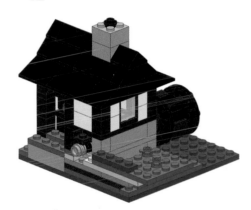

13

14

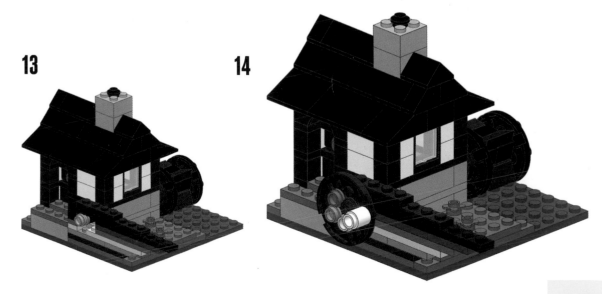

observatory

Gazing up into the night sky has been a fascination since time began. Over the years, as the technology of telescopes has advanced, so too have the buildings that house them. Observatory roofs are usually dome-shaped with a section that can open. This model uses 3 × 3 × 2 dome corner bricks to create this traditional shape. A click hinge in the gap left between the corner bricks allows the telescope to angle up and down.

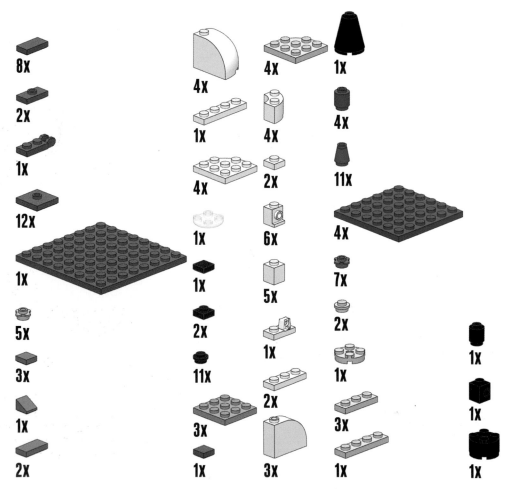

8x

2x

1x

12x

1x

5x

3x

1x

2x

4x

1x

4x

1x

1x

2x

11x

3x

1x

4x

4x

2x

6x

5x

1x

2x

3x

3x

1x

4x

11x

4x

7x

2x

1x

3x

1x

1x

1x

1x

OBSERVATORY

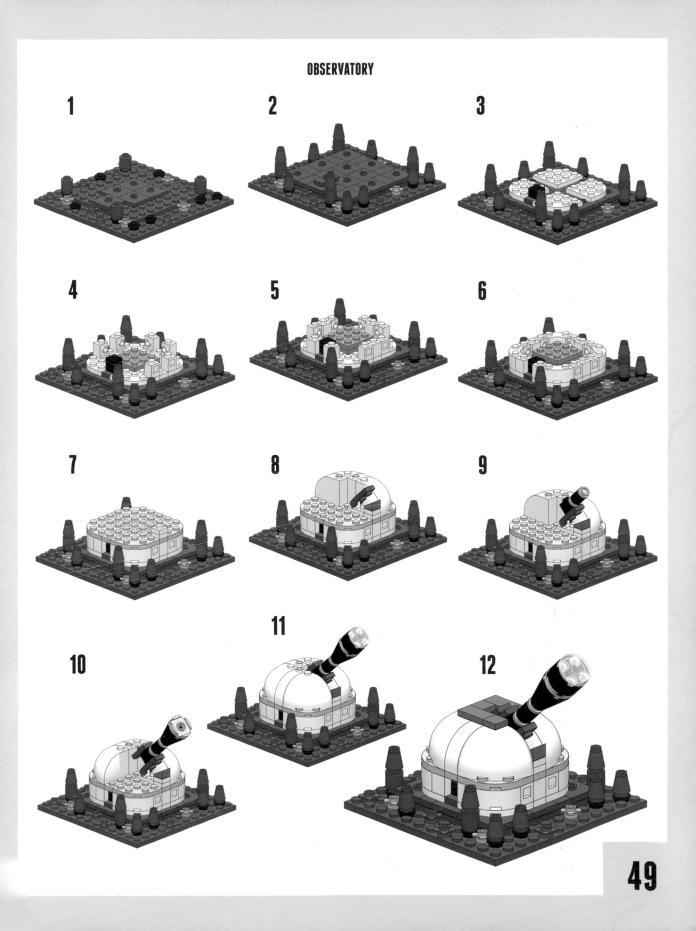

igloo

Way up in the Arctic circle, people built igloos to stay out of harsh weather. They were built using blocks carved from snow. Tiny air pockets in the snow acted as insulation. Even when the temperature reached -49°F (-45°C) outside, it could have been up to 61°F (16°C) on the inside, warmed by body heat alone. Offsetting plates using jumpers gives the structure a gently curved effect without using curved slopes.

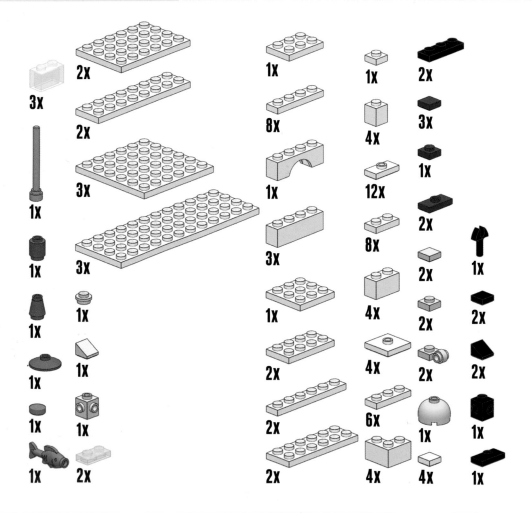

3x 2x

1x 2x

1x 3x

1x 3x

1x

1x

1x 1x

1x 1x

1x 2x

1x 1x 2x 2x

8x 3x 4x

1x 12x

1x 2x 8x 2x 1x

1x 4x 2x 2x

2x 4x 2x 2x

2x 6x 1x 1x

2x 4x 4x 1x

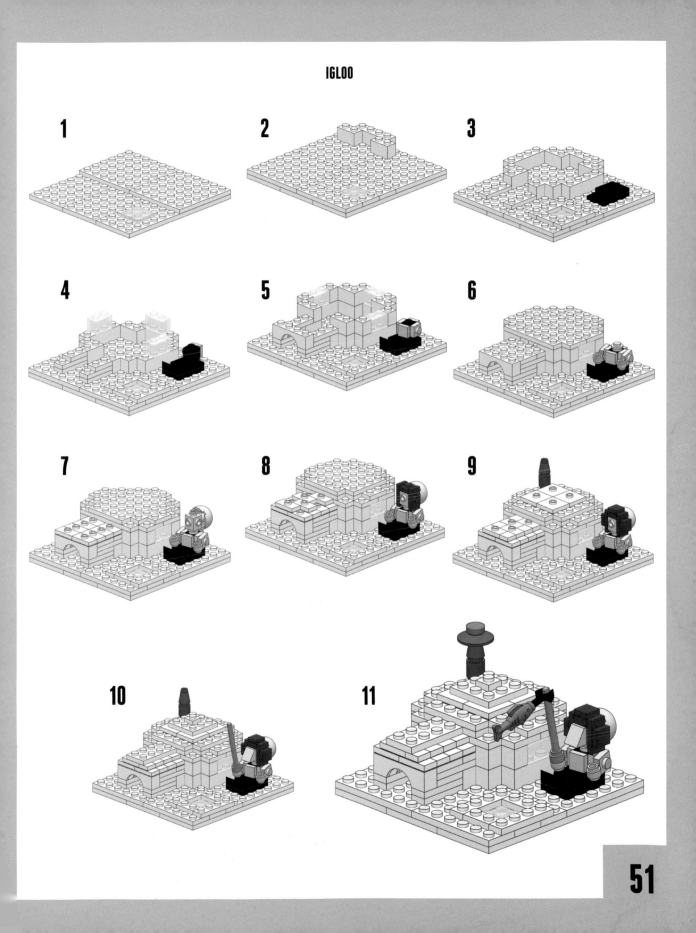

1 **2** **3**

4 **5** **6**

7 **8** **9**

10 **11**

shoe house

There was an old woman who lived in a shoe ... so, why shouldn't others follow her example and turn a shoe into a home? The shoelace is made using modified tiles with grills, with a horn clipped on upside down for the ends. The shoe's distinctive shape is made using 2 × 3 inverted slopes to give the arch in front of the heel, and a 4 × 3 wedge slope is used for the toe.

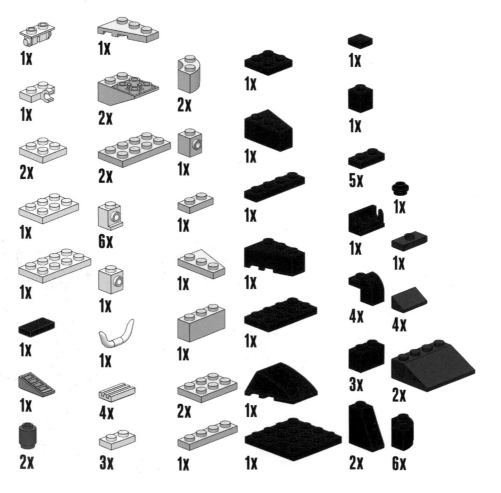

SHOE HOUSE

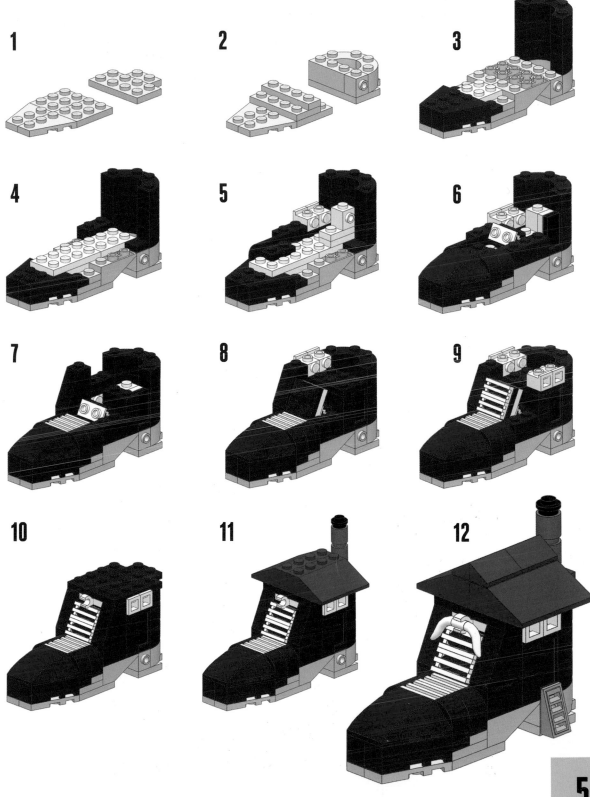

stilt house

Houses aren't just built on stilts to keep water out (see page 38), they are also used in hot countries where the circulating air underneath helps to keep the house cool. Plus, stilts make it much more difficult for mice and rats to get in. The two different colors of orange used for the roof make it look like it's made out of old iron.

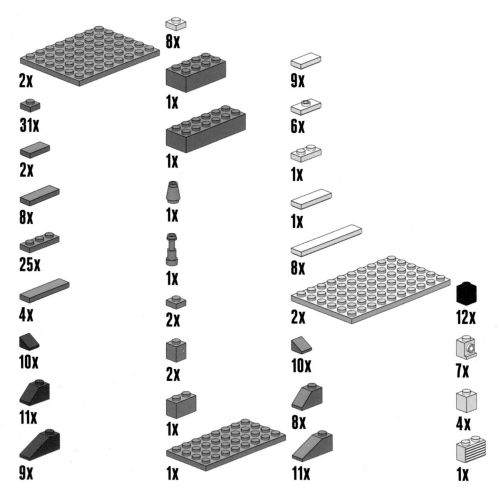

2x · 8x · 9x

31x · 1x · 6x

2x · 1x · 1x

8x · 1x · 1x

25x · 1x · 8x

4x · 2x · 2x · 12x

10x · 2x · 10x · 7x

11x · 1x · 8x · 4x

9x · 1x · 11x · 1x

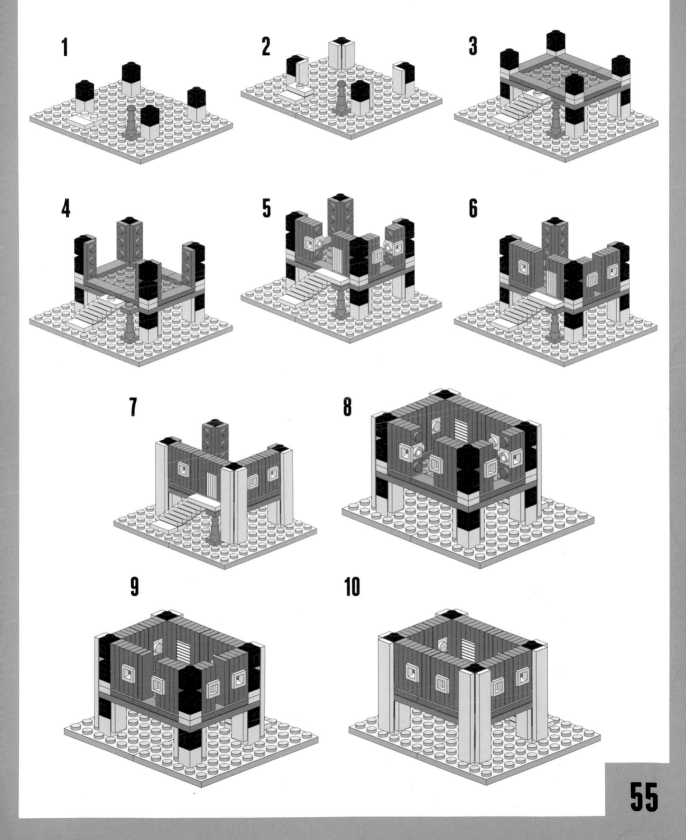

11

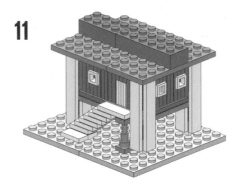

12

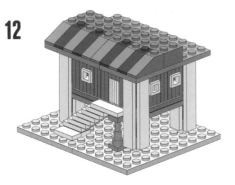

13

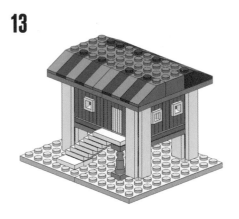

14

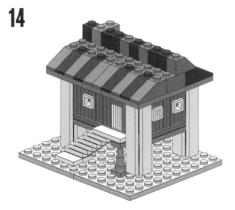

15

16

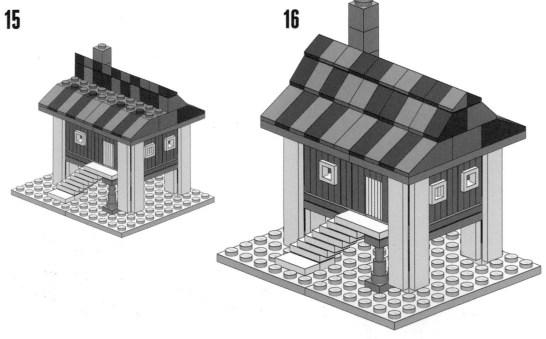

rickety shack

With holes in the roof and boarded up windows, this is one old and rickety shack. Left to the mercy of the wind and rain, most buildings gradually fall to pieces until they're barely held together at all. Using black plates under the loose roof tiles makes it look as if there are big holes in the roof, and the different colored 1 × 2 tiles look like mismatched and fading panels on the walls.

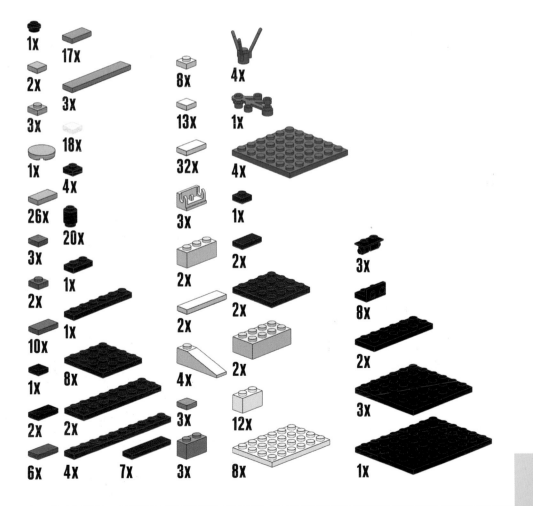

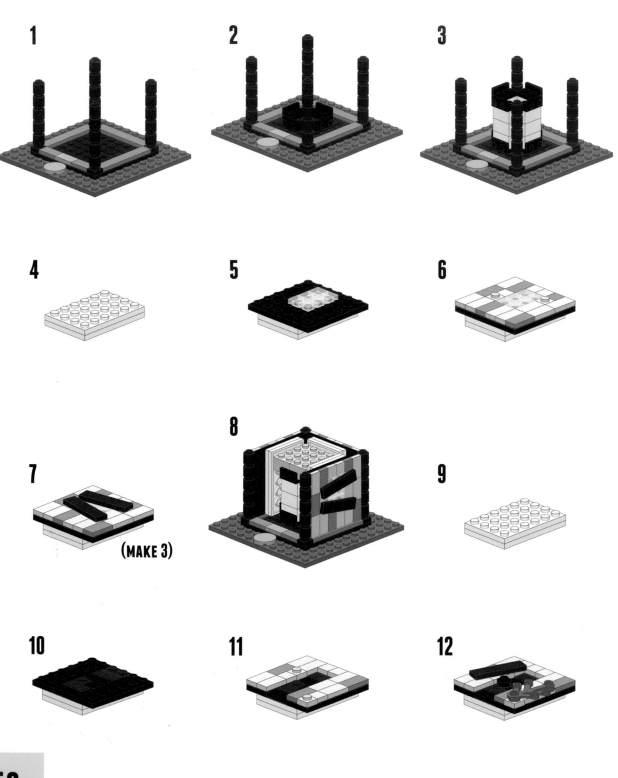

1

2

3

4

5

6

7

(MAKE 3)

8

9

10

11

12

13

14

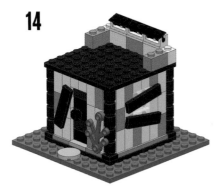

15

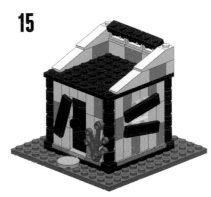

16

17

18

round house

Many years ago, all across Europe, people lived in round houses. They had a simple and sturdy design, usually made of stone or wooden posts joined together, topped with a conical grass roof. I've used 2 × 2 round corner bricks, which are also known as Macaroni Bricks, to give the building its round appearance. A selection of round corner plates and round plates stacked on top of each other make the roof.

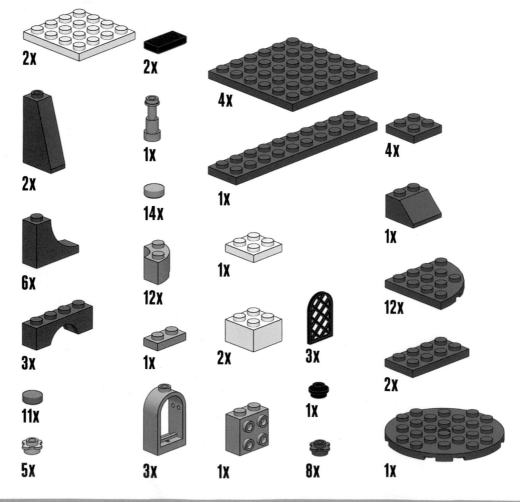

2x

2x

4x

4x

2x

1x

1x

1x

6x

14x

1x

12x

1x

12x

3x

1x

2x

3x

2x

11x

1x

5x

3x

1x

8x

1x

ROUND HOUSE

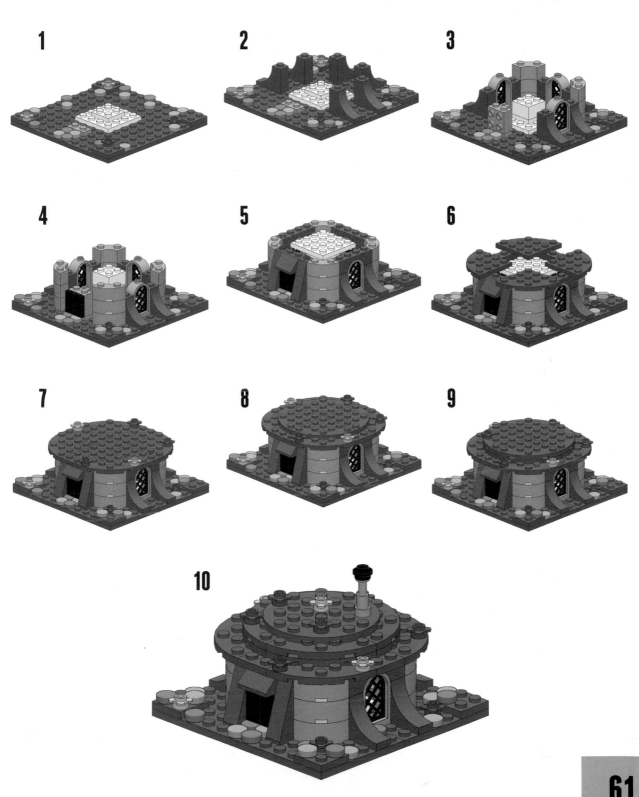

treasure keep

Long ago, when invading armies stole from other lands, people needed somewhere very safe to store their treasures. They built treasure keeps, which were extremely strong structures, usually placed at the heart of a castle. The distinctive arrow loops at the base of this treasure keep are made using 1 × 1 tan tiles turned on their sides, while a 4 × 2 black, spindled fence placed on jumper plates makes a great iron-barred window at the top of the keep.

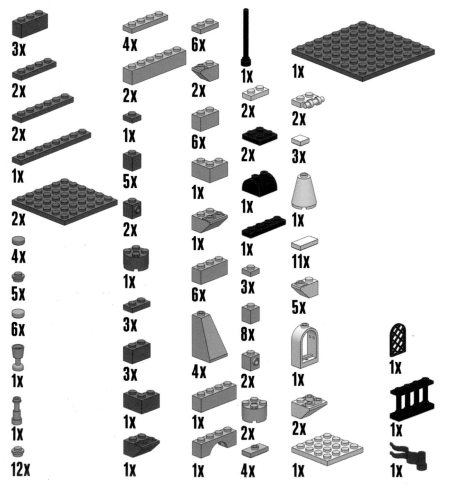

TREASURE KEEP

1

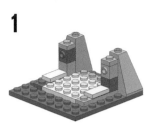

2

3

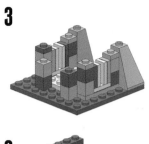

4

5

6

7

8

9

10

11

12

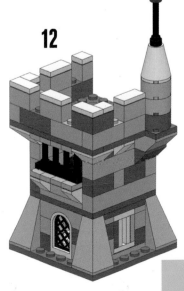

wacky wagon

When people set out to the Wild West of America in the 1800s, they traveled in wagons. As motor engines were developed, some people combined their traditional wagons with modern engines, leading to some interesting designs. All the bright colors used in this model add to its wackiness. The traditional big wagon wheels are made using 4 × 4 round plates attached to 2 × 2 round plates.

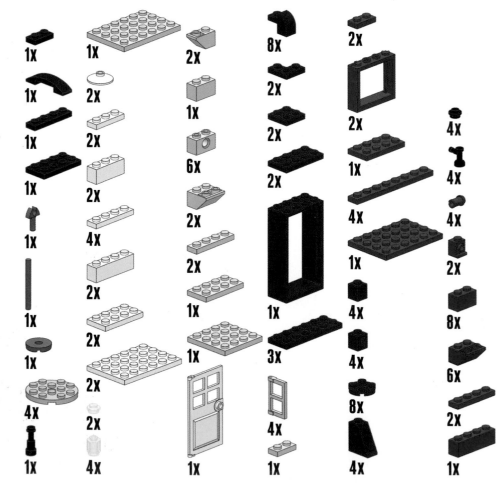

WACKY WAGON

1

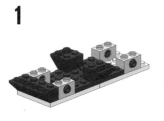

2

3

4

5

6

7

8

9

10

11

12

troll cave

In fairy tales, caves are popular places for villains to live, which is the inspiration for the troll in this model. The inverted slopes support the roof without losing space inside. The animal skull at the opening is made from two claws and a curved slope, attached with a headlight brick.

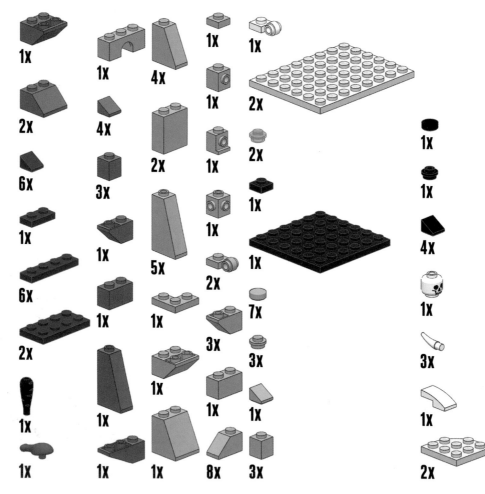

TROLL CAVE

1

2

3
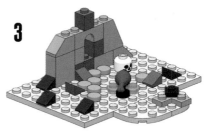

4

5
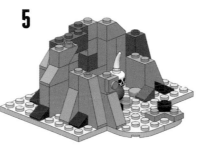

6
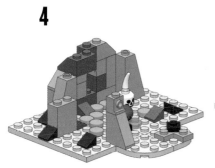

7

8

9

10

11

12
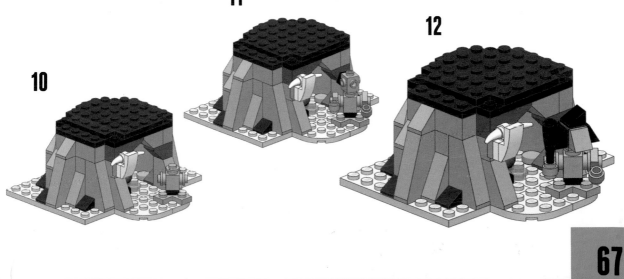

lighthouse

Many ships have been saved from crashing into rocks by the lighthouses positioned around coastlines. Although they're mainly automatic now, they used to be operated by a lighthouse keeper who lived in a house attached to the tower. The building's unique look is made using 2 × 2 round tiles with holes in the middle, which allow for the large cone brick to be placed upside-down to support the light.

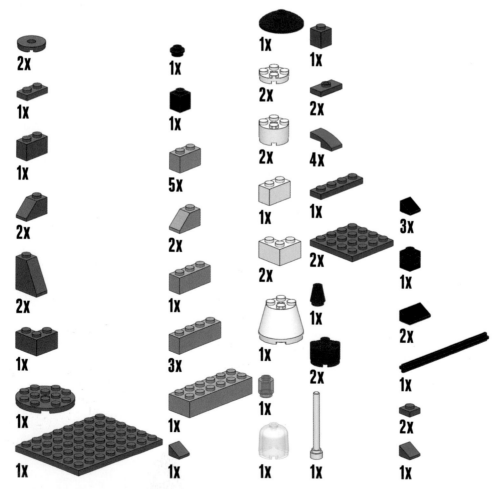

2x

1x

1x

2x

2x

1x

1x

1x

1x

1x

5x

2x

1x

3x

1x

1x

1x

2x

2x

2x

1x

2x

1x

1x

2x

1x

1x

1x

1x

1x

2x

4x

1x

2x

2x

1x

2x

1x

3x

1x

2x

1x

2x

1x

LIGHTHOUSE

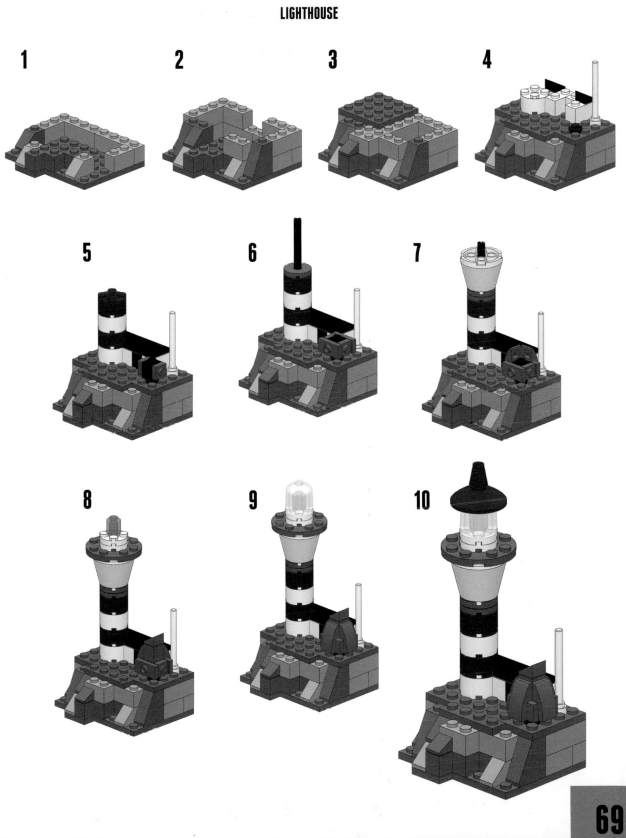

giant egg house

Living in a giant egg would be nice and cozy. Due to the shape, you could easily have two floors and a great view. To create the egg shape, the lowest level has a shallower curve than the higher levels, which are steeper. These traditional window boxes have been made using fence pieces, but if you don't have any, you could use flowers instead.

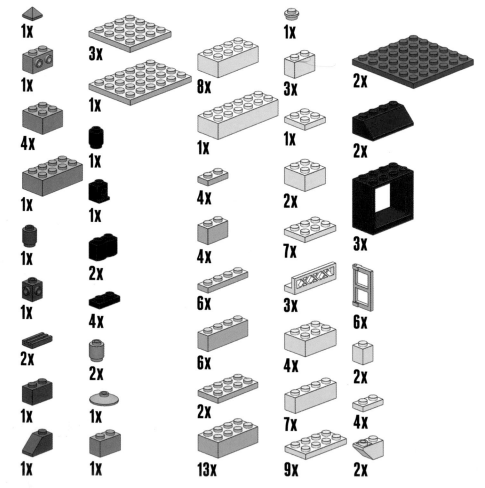

GIANT EGG HOUSE

1

2

3
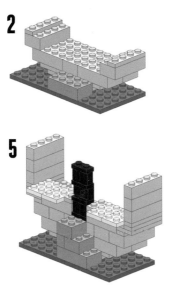

4

5
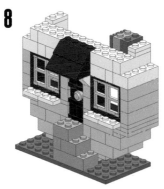

6
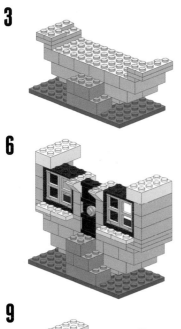

7

8
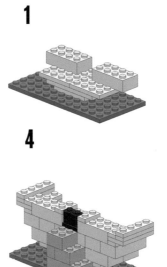

9

10

11

12

dragon's lair

There are many stories about dragons who live in hidden lairs where they guard their precious treasures of gold and silver. Dragons build their lairs in secluded places, such as in caves or deep in the woods. This one is in an old, ruined building. The treasure chest uses 1 x 2 hinge bricks so it can be opened. Gold and silver 1 x 1 tiles make perfect coins.

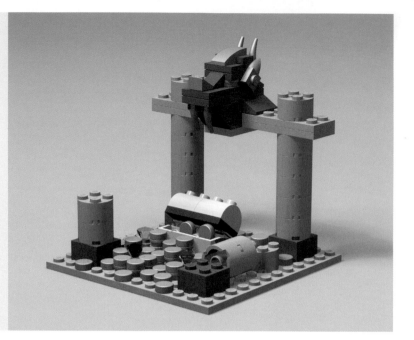

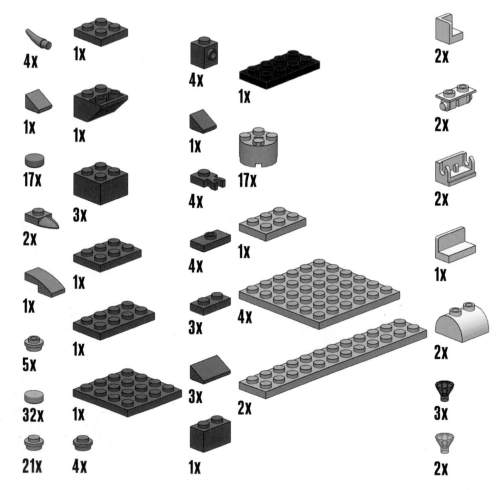

4x
1x
4x
1x
2x

1x
1x
1x
17x
2x

17x
4x
2x

2x
3x
4x
2x

1x
4x
1x
1x

1x
3x
4x
2x

5x
1x
3x
2x
3x

32x
1x
2x

21x
4x
1x
2x

DRAGON'S LAIR

1

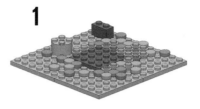

2

3

4

5

6

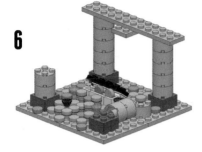

7

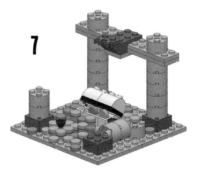

8

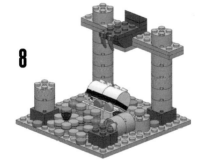

9

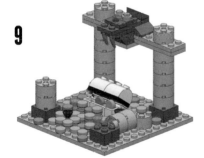

10

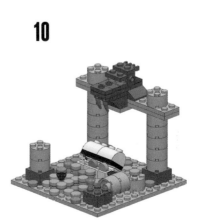

11

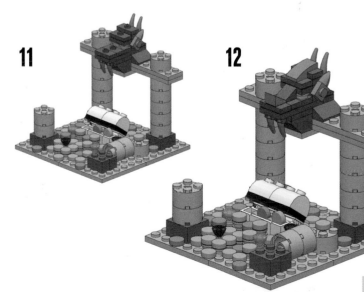

12

mountain fortress

Up in the rocky crags of a mountain sits this fortress, with its high walls and winding path to the main entrance. Usually built on an outcrop of solid rock, these fortresses were made for defense, using the steep mountain slopes as a natural barrier. Slope bricks of different heights are used to create the steep, sloping mountainsides.

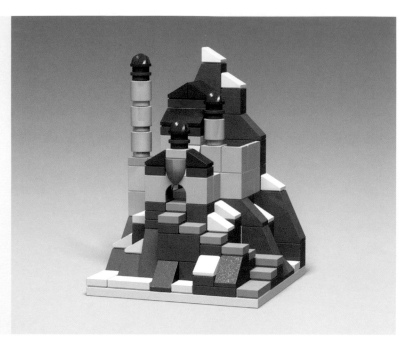

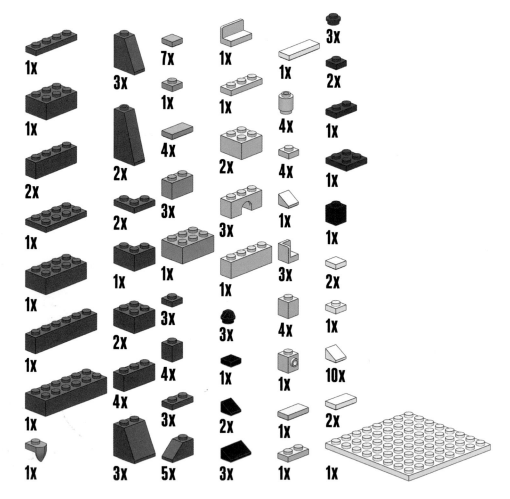

MOUNTAIN FORTRESS

1
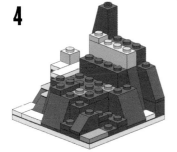

2
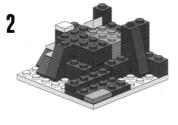

3
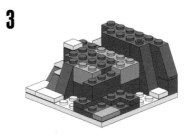

4
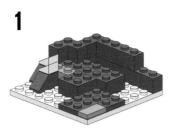

5
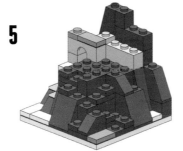

6

7
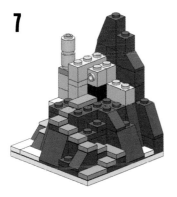

8
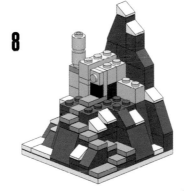

9
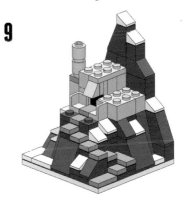

10
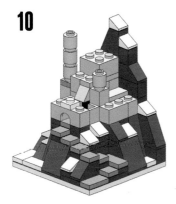

11
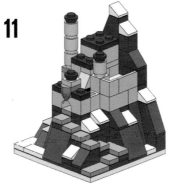

12
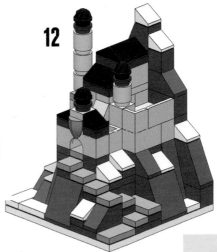

tropical hideaway

Imagine if beaches weren't just for vacations and you could live on one all the time, listening to the gentle rhythm of the waves while relaxing under a canopy of palm trees. Many indigenous coastal people use palm leaves to make roofs that keep out the tropical rain. I've used curved bricks for the palm leaves. For the low walls of the structure, I've used tiles with grilles attached to minifigure neck brackets turned upside down.

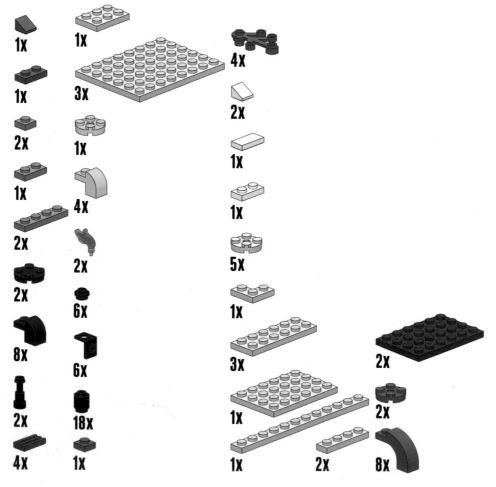

1X 1X 4X

1X 3X 2X

2X 1X 1X

1X 4X 1X

2X 2X 5X

2X 6X 1X

8X 6X 3X 2X

2X 18X 1X 2X

4X 1X 1X 2X 8X

TROPICAL HIDEAWAY

1

2

3

4

5

6

7

8

9

10

11

12

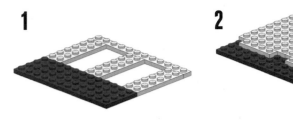

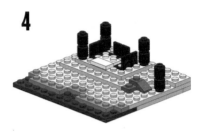
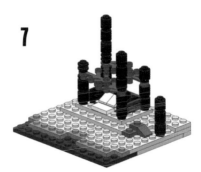
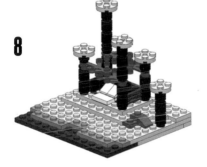
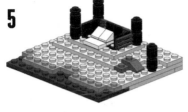

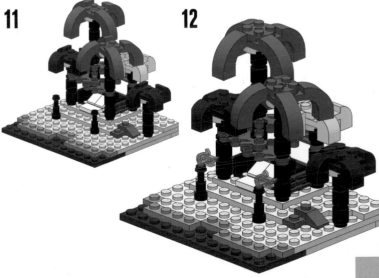

glass house

Why spoil a great view with solid walls when you can build walls out of glass? Some real houses have rooms built almost completely with glass, so it can feel as if you are living in a garden. I've gone one step further and built the whole house out of transparent bricks—some clear and some light blue to add a touch of color to the glass house.

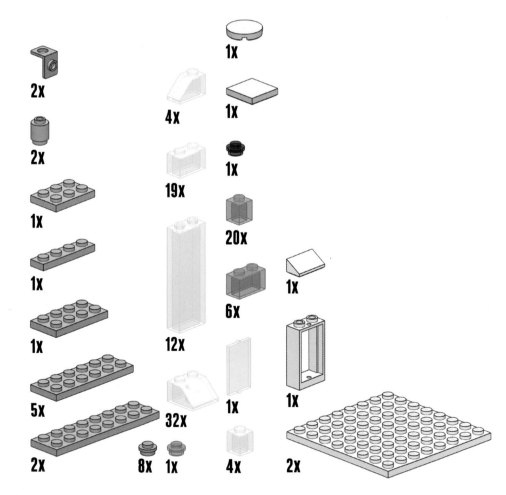

2x

2x

1x

1x

1x

5x

2x

4x

19x

12x

32x

8x 1x

1x

1x

20x

6x

1x

4x

1x

1x

1x

1x

2x

GLASS HOUSE

1

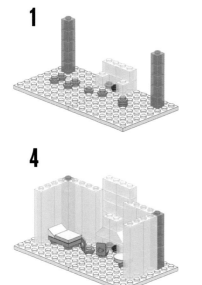

2

3

4

5

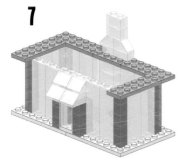

6

7

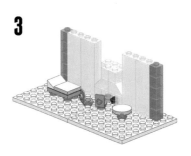

8

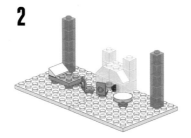

9

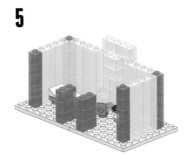

10

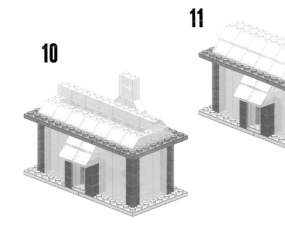

11

12

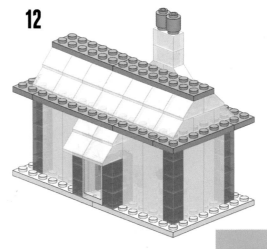

mushroom house

Some people think fairies live in mushrooms. And in some fairy tales there are tiny villages created completely from big and small mushroom houses. The tiny windows are 1 x 1 headlight bricks turned sideways. You can make your mushroom house feel even more magical by using round 1 x 1 glow-in-the-dark plates for the spots on top. Just turn off the lights and watch it glow.

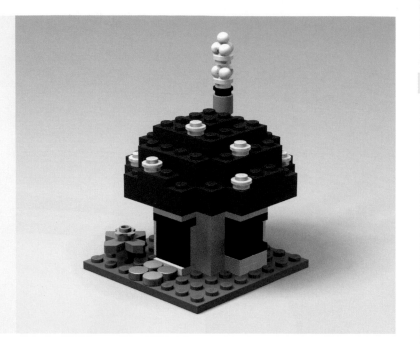

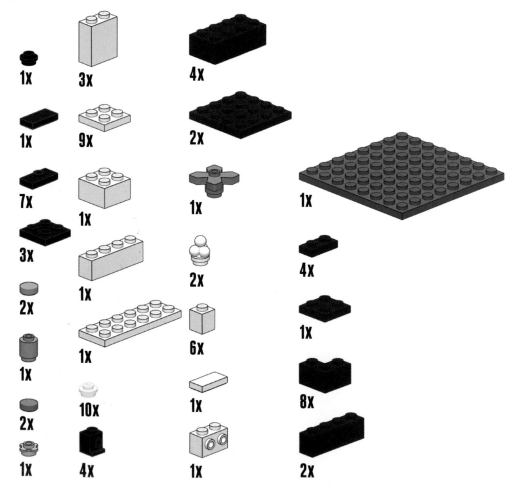

1x 3x 4x
1x 9x 2x
7x 1x 1x 1x
3x 1x 2x 4x
2x 1x 1x
1x 1x 6x
2x 10x 1x 8x
1x 4x 1x 2x

MUSHROOM HOUSE

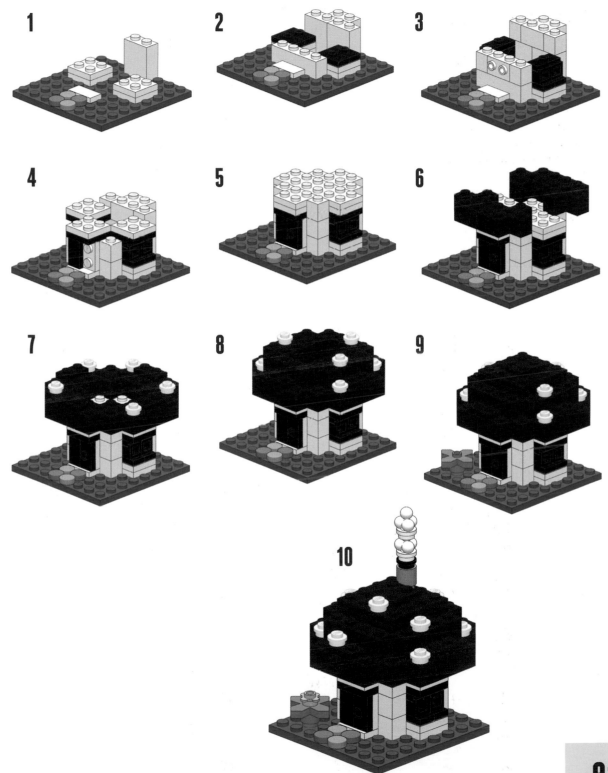

giant shell

Imagine you lived at the bottom of the ocean. Where better to make your home than in a giant shell? Add some windows, and just sit back and watch the fish swim past your living room. The curved slopes I have used here are perfect for creating the ridges on the shell.

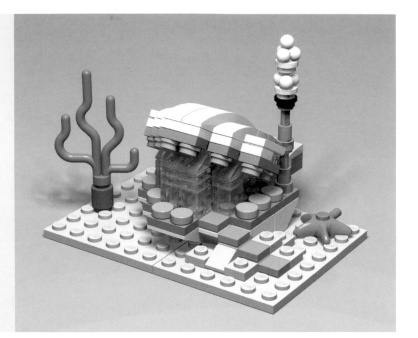

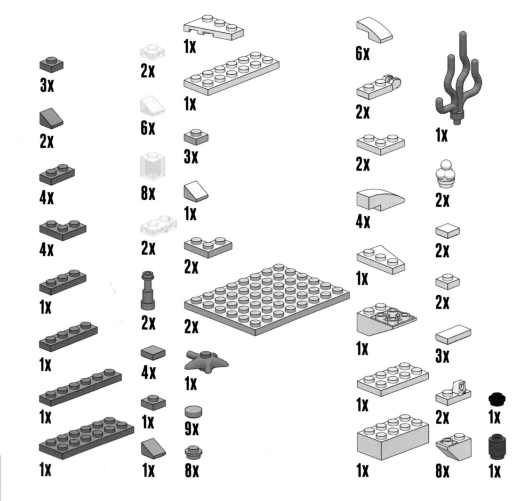

3x

2x

4x

4x

1x

1x

1x

1x

2x

6x

3x

8x

1x

2x

2x

4x

1x

1x

2x

2x

1x

1x

2x

1x

9x

8x

6x

2x

2x

2x

4x

1x

1x

1x

2x

1x

6x

1x

2x

2x

3x

2x

1x

8x

1x

82

GIANT SHELL

1

2

3

4

5

6

7

8

9

10

11

pumpkin house

If Cinderella's fairy godmother can turn a pumpkin into a carriage, why shouldn't you turn one into a house? Living in a pumpkin could be quite roomy, as they are one of the larger fruits. I've used 1 × 1 slopes attached sideways to give the pumpkin a rounder look.

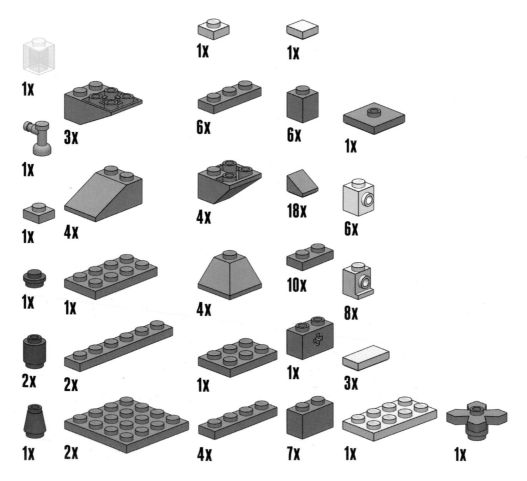

PUMPKIN HOUSE

1

2

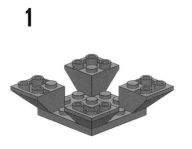

3

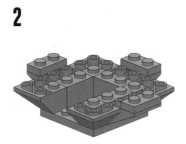

4

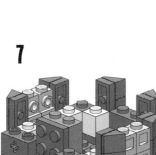

5

(MAKE 6)

6

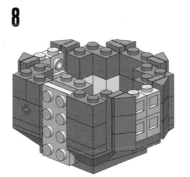

7

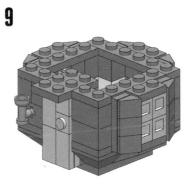

8

9

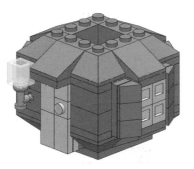

10

11

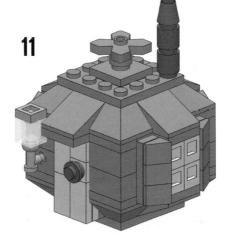

volcano shack

Some scientists live next to live volcanoes so that they can monitor their activity. They hope to learn more about volcanoes so that they can give early warnings to save the lives of people living nearby. It can get pretty hot—and dangerous—living there. The transparent orange slopes and tiles create the red hot lava flowing past the shack.

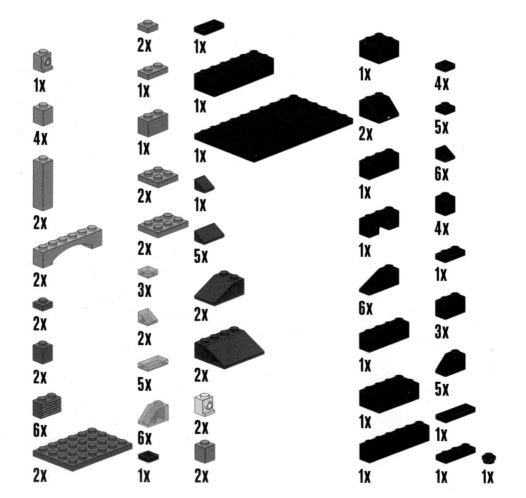

VOLCANO SHACK

1

2

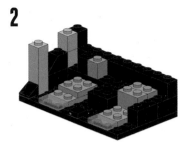

3

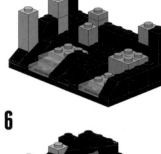

4

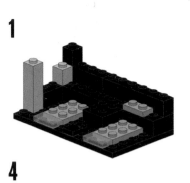

5

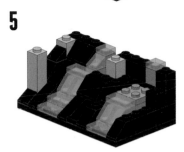

6

7

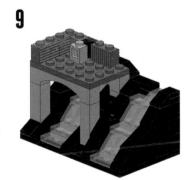

8

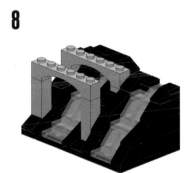

9

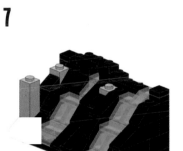

10

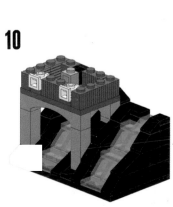

11

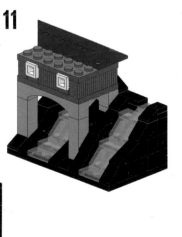

12

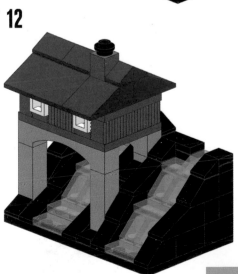

windmill

Windmills harness the wind to turn giant sails. They have existed for centuries and used to be the miller's home and place of work. Over the years, they have been used for everything from pumping water out of low lying land to grinding flour. Now there are wind turbines that are used for making electricity. This windmill has sails made from fences attached to studs. I've placed a 2 × 2 turntable plate between the top of the model and the base so the windmill can turn to face the wind.

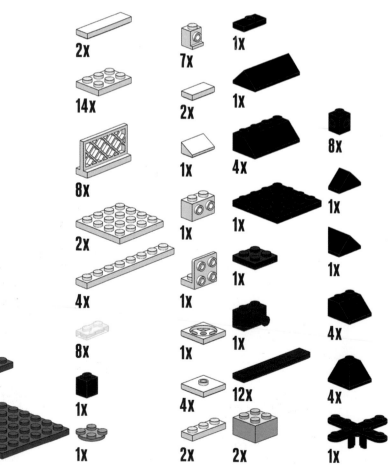

7x

4x

1x

4x

1x

2x

1x

1x

2x

14x

8x

2x

4x

8x

1x

1x

7x

2x

1x

4x

1x

1x

1x

4x

1x

12x

2x

1x

1x

1x

1x

1x

8x

1x

4x

4x

1x

2x

WINDMILL

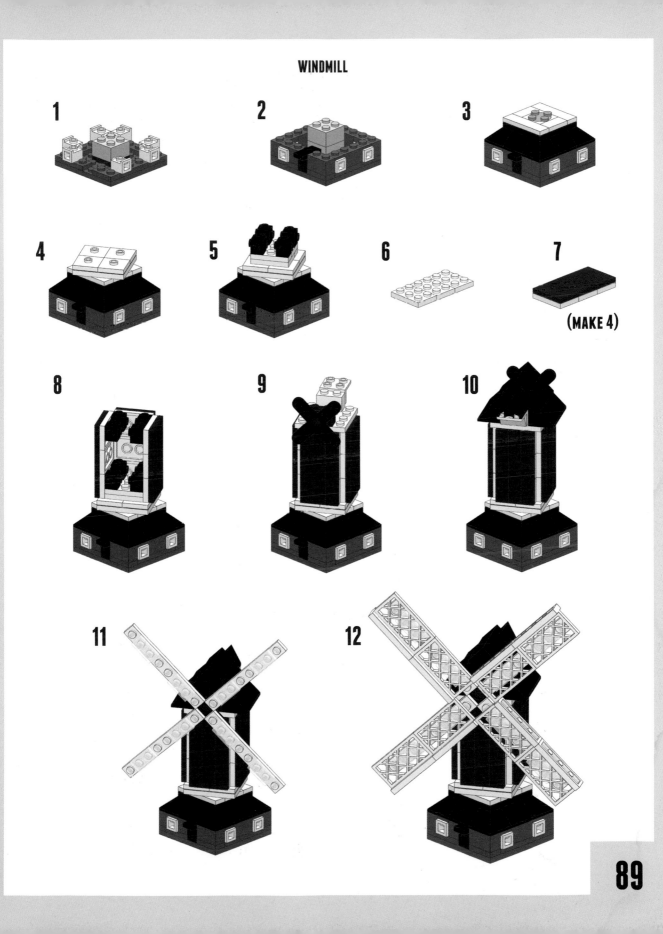

tree house

Many backyards have tree houses. They are often nestled in the crook of a trunk and a branch, but they can be expanded so people can actually live in them. In some rainforests, people live high up in the trees to keep safe from dangers at ground level. They even take their pets up there with them. The 2 × 2 × 3 slopes make a strong base for this tree house. Tiles are attached to headlight bricks to create the wood panels.

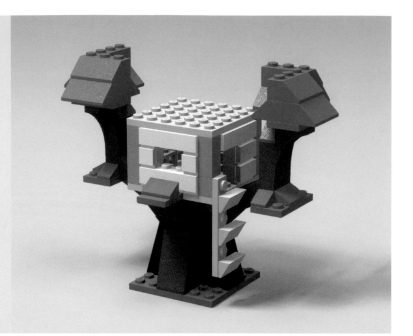

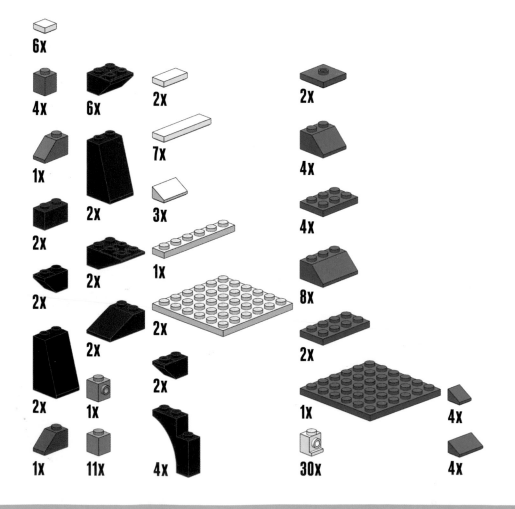

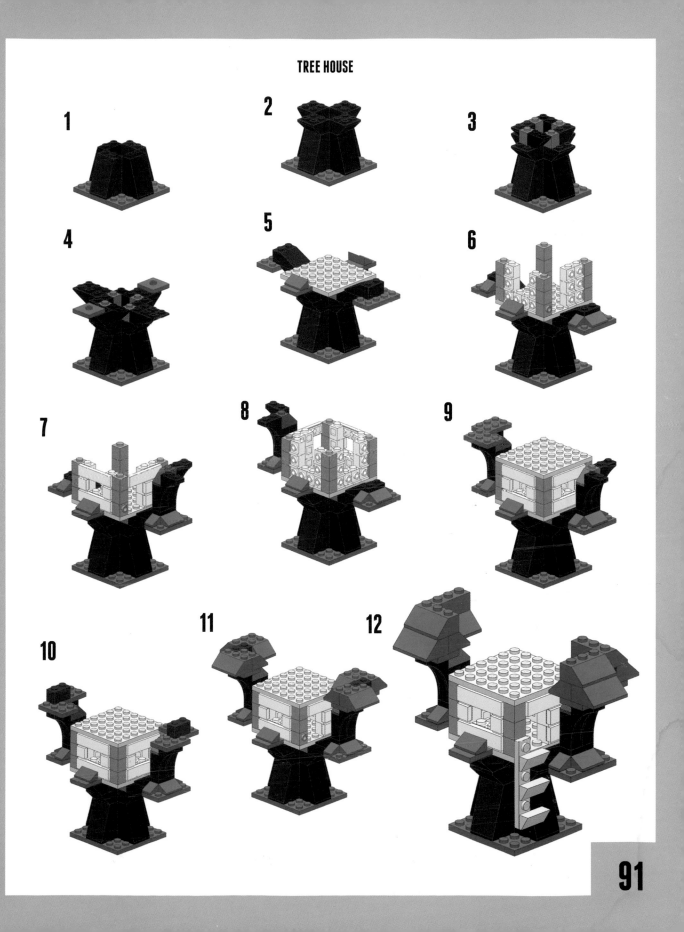

underground home

Since the Stone Age, some people have lived in caves for shelter. Sometimes it was to get away from the heat, but other times it was to stay warm. Using various tones of tan, dark orange, and reddish brown creates the different layers of the earth, and 1 × 1 round bricks with a reddish brown lightsaber blade create the tree roots under the ground.

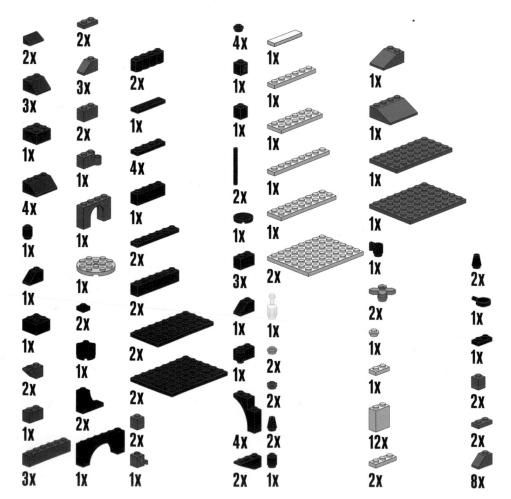

UNDERGROUND HOME

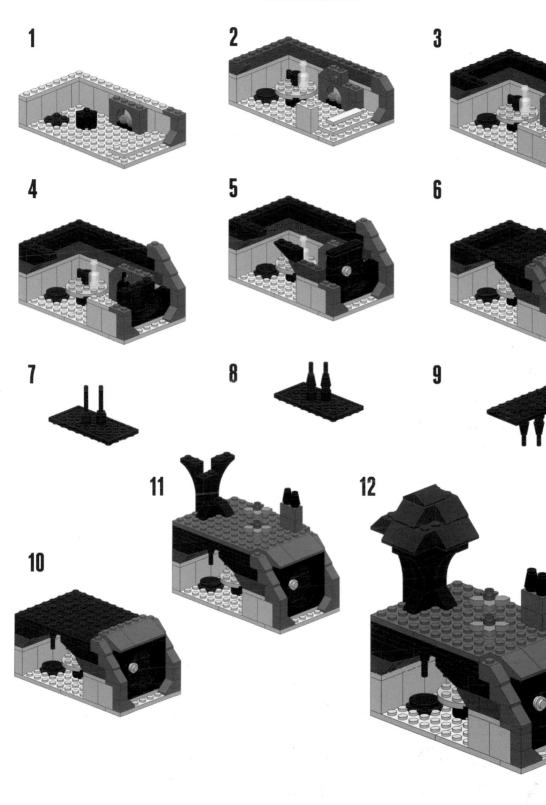

ice castle

Ice castles aren't only in fairy tales. In countries such as Canada and Sweden, there are hotels made completely out of ice. They melt when the warmer weather comes and have to be rebuilt every year. The mix of clear and transparent light blue bricks give this ice castle definition. Its fabulous main entrance is made using transparent light blue 1 x 1 slopes on their sides, attached to clear headlight bricks.

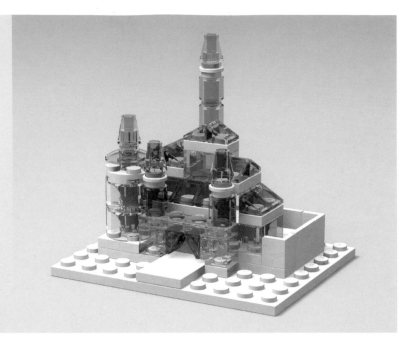

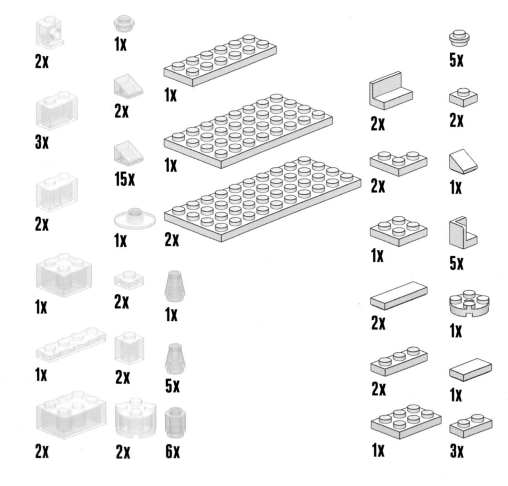

ICE CASTLE

1

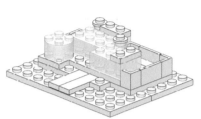

2

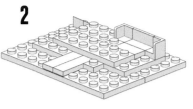

3

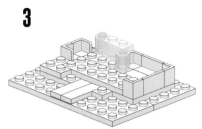

4

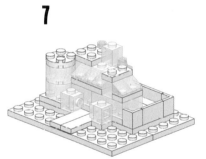

5

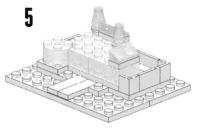

6

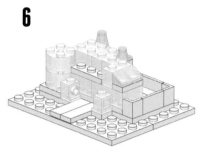

7

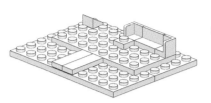

8

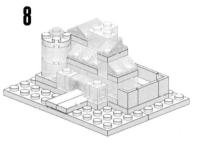

9

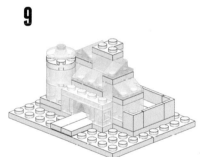

11

10

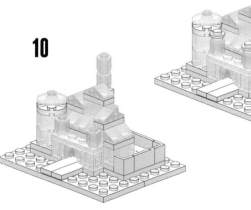

12

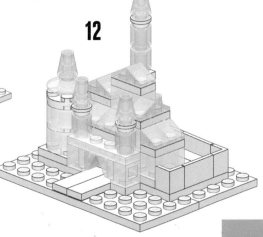

credits

Kevin Hall is a cofounder of Brick Galleria—a LEGO® brick model building design and events company—and a professional LEGO brick artist. He designs, develops, and creates LEGO brick models for companies, events, promotions, and collectors. He has been part of the international LEGO community since 2000, creating models and sculptures and designing custom collector figurines, bespoke sets, graphics, and promotional material for events around the world. His models have been featured in television advertising campaigns, toy fairs, exhibitions, print media, and theme parks, and have been used by government organizations. He recently turned his hand to writing and his work was featured in the official LEGO book, *365 Things to Do with LEGO Bricks,* which won the "Best Book" category in the Creative Play Awards 2016 in the United Kingdom. He also organizes and runs LEGO workshops for children and corporate groups. Before becoming a professional LEGO brick artist, Kevin spent three decades in the advertising industry in various creative incarnations.

Brenda Tsang is a cofounder of Brick Galleria. This followed fifteen years of creating and managing products for global entertainment brands. Brenda is passionate about creating products that have cutting-edge functionality, are aesthetically pleasing, and stand out from the crowd. She also specializes in scenery art and spatial design, which enables her to create the enhanced experience of Brick Galleria events. Brenda helped on the research and design for models in this book and with selecting LEGO parts for some of the finer details.

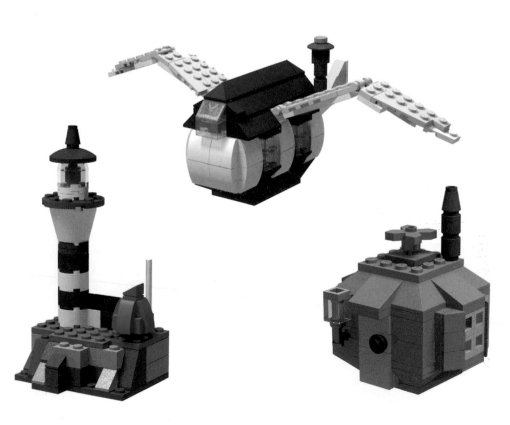